Troubleshoot

OTHER TITLES BY THE SAME AUTHOR

Troubleshooting your PC

by

Ian Sinclair

BERNARD BABANI (publishing) LTD
THE GRAMPIANS
SHEPHERDS BUSH ROAD
LONDON W6 7NF
ENGLAND

PLEASE NOTE

Although every care has been taken with the production of this book to ensure that any projects, designs, modifications and/or programs, etc., contained herewith, operate in a correct and safe manner and also that any components specified are normally available in Great Britain, the Publishers and Author(s) do not accept responsibility in any way for the failure (including fault in design) of any project, design, modification or program to work correctly or to cause damage to any equipment that it may be connected to or used in conjunction with, or in respect of any other damage or injury that may be so caused, nor do the Publishers accept responsibility in any way for the failure to obtain specified components.

Notice is also given that if equipment that is still under warranty is modified in any way or used or connected with home-built equipment then that warranty may be void.

© 1997 BERNARD BABANI (publishing) LTD

First Published – December 1997
Reprinted – November 1998

British Library Cataloguing in Publication Data:
A catalogue record for this book is available from the British Library

ISBN 0 85934 439 8

Cover Design by Gregor Arthur
Cover illustration by Adam Willis
Printed and bound in Great Britain by Cox & Wyman Ltd, Reading

Preface

The PC is a remarkably reliable machine, and you should not think after reading this book that you might be facing hundreds of possible disasters. Nevertheless, there are a lot of things that can go wrong, proving the truth of the old maxim that anything that can go wrong will do so at some time.

Most PC users, particularly new users, suspect the hardware when something goes wrong, but the cause is very much more often the software. In this book, both the hardware and the software are considered, and we look at what can go wrong, how it affects the PC, and what to do about it. One important point to remember is that both the hardware and the software are subject to constant revision, so that some potential flaws are eliminated but others can appear.

This is therefore not a long list of symptoms and causes, because these change as fast as versions of your software and hardware. The aim of this book is to show you how to find the cause of faults and where to look for detailed information; it's like providing seeds rather than food.

There are some faults that can be remedied with very little skill or knowledge, some that need a little more understanding. The hardware of the computer itself is not mechanically or electrically difficult to work on, needing little more than two screwdrivers (one plain, one Philips) and a pair of pliers. Anyone who was brought up on a Meccano set, or a modern equivalent, should be able to work on a defunct computer.

The monitor and the printer, however, are no-go areas, difficult to work on and with hazards for the inexperienced. The monitor in particular, has dangerous voltages at points inside the casing, and the casing must not be removed unless you happen to be experienced in TV repairs.

Software tips are mainly concerned with Windows 95 and Windows 98, since this is the software that every PC modern machine is certain to use, though some older machines will still be using Windows 3.1 or 3.11. There are some programs that are notorious for causing problems, but they are likely to be out of use, or rewritten by the time this book appears.

My hope is that the use of this book will for some readers at least, minimise the impact of that moment when the hard drive does not start, the printer produces gibberish, or when the screen suddenly goes blank. None of this, however, obviates the need to keep backups of all your valuable data and programs. A good backup system is your first line of defence, because it ensures that even if your PC suffered total meltdown your really valuable material (which cannot be insured) will be safe.

One potential source of problems has been omitted. This book does not deal with networked computers, because the problems that can be encountered using networks would require a book to themselves of many times this size. Many networking problems require the attention of an expert and considerable help from the supplier of the network, whereas this book has been directed at the owner-user of the computer, and particularly applies to one-off desktop machines.

- Throughout the book, the abbreviations Kbyte, Mbyte and Gbyte have been used for memory size and disc capacity figures. These refer to capacities that are graded in steps of 1024, so that:
  1024 bytes = 1 Kbyte
  1024 Kbyte = 1 Mbyte
  1024 Mbyte = 1 Gbyte
  On this basis, the capacity of a floppy disc is 1.4 Mbyte rather than the 1.44 that is often quoted.

The book is not aimed at any particular age or occupation of PC user, and I should remind young readers that notes on making repairs to the inside of a PC assume that you know the elements of electrical safety. If in doubt, always work under supervision.

No single book can be a substitute for experience in this respect, and I urge each reader to subscribe to a good PC magazine and to keep a paper file of the hints that appear each month. This allows you to build up a collection of useful tips that will help when you encounter an elusive problem.

The points that are covered in this book are intended to be relevant to PC machines old and new, with particular reference to machines that by now will be well out of guarantee time.

Ian Sinclair

Summer 1997

ABOUT THE AUTHOR

Ian Sinclair was born in 1932 in Tayport, Fife, and graduated from the University of St. Andrews in 1956. In that year, he joined the English Electric Valve Co. in Chelmsford, Essex, to work on the design of specialised cathode-ray tubes, and later on small transmitting valves and TV transmitting tubes.

In 1966, he became an assistant lecturer at Hornchurch Technical College, and in 1967 joined the staff of Braintree College of F.E. as a lecturer. His first book, "Understanding Electronic Components" was published in 1972, and he has been writing ever since, particularly for the novice in Electronics or Computing. The interest in computing arose after seeing a Tandy TRS80 in San Francisco in 1977, and of his 180 published books, about half have been on computing topics, starting with a guide to Microsoft Basic on the TRS80 in 1979.

He left teaching in 1984 to concentrate entirely on writing, and has also gained experience in computer typesetting, particularly for mathematical texts. He has recently visited Seattle to see Microsoft at work, and to remind them that he has been using Microsoft products longer than most Microsoft employees can remember.

ACKNOWLEDGEMENTS

I would like to thank the staff of Text 100 Ltd. for providing the Windows 95 software which is so frequently mentioned in the course of this book.

TRADEMARKS

Microsoft, MS-DOS, Windows, Windows 95 and NT are either registered trademarks or trademarks of Microsoft Corporation.

All other brand and product names used in this book are recognised as trademarks, or registered trademarks, of their respective companies.

CONTENTS

1 Hardware or software

A fault might be caused by software or by hardware, and it's important (and often difficult) to tell which of these is the cause. Some hardware faults are obvious, such as no sound from a hard drive, but others are more dubious — there are, for example, software faults or incorrect settings that can prevent a floppy drive or CD-ROM drive from operating.

In addition, modern computer motherboards are festooned with detection points that can check the chip temperature, case temperature, fan speed and other factors and shut the computer down if there is any risk. Like car burglar alarms, there is always a prospect that one of these safeguards will give a false warning.

We start, then, with a **very** rough guide to classifying a fault as hardware or software, remembering that a computer is controlled totally by its software. For example, if you have just had the case open to add a drive, add memory, or alter settings it would seem foolish to suspect a software fault if the machine did not restart correctly. On the other hand, it might simply be that the machine is responding by requiring you to enter the changes you have made into the CMOS RAM.

Typical hardware faults

No 'on' light when you switch on

No sound from the hard drive(s)

Nothing appearing on monitor

Floppy drive light stays on

Typical software faults

Machine hangs up, keys have no effect

Machine keeps rebooting

Troubleshooting your PC

Files cannot be read from drives

Machine reports system fault

Typical faults that can be of either or both types

Floppy drive fails in copy action

No sound

Garbage on monitor

Garbage from printer

Noisy hard drive

Obvious reasons

To save time and space, we'll dispose of some obvious reasons for failure to start. These are items that are not so likely to stop the PC working in mid-session, because you would be aware of the cause.

- Power failure or power switched off, either at the wall socket or on the computer or monitor.

- Power or external connecting cables pulled out.

- Fuse blown in mains plug or (less likely) inside the computer.

We assume that you will have checked these items or that you know they are not a cause of the problem.

Know your PC

You are at a considerable advantage if you have been using the same PC for some time, perhaps a year or more. That way, you have become accustomed to what is normal, and you are more likely to detect something unusual. This is, of course, no consolation to the owner of a fairly new machine who has not had time to get to know its peculiarities, and certainly no help if you have had only a few hours with your first-ever PC.

Hardware or software?

On the other hand, a new machine is still under guarantee and though machines can be, and are, delivered with faults, this is not common. The normal experience, in fact, is to have a totally trouble-free life from a PC from the time you buy it to the time you part with it. Complications arise mainly if you install and remove a large number of programs, which is why PCs belonging to technical journalists often provide exercises in fault-finding software problems. Another cause of (hardware) faults is shoddy work in replacing a drive or adding equipment. These are routine tasks that should not cause problems, but there will always be a time when a connector is replaced the wrong way round or a new chunk of memory is defective from the start.

What did you do?

When something goes wrong, it's important to remember what you did. It's not so easy as it sounds, because you don't go around making notes about each action; it's like trying to produce an alibi for the 14th of December 1996. Unless you have some particular reason to remember what you did, it's not easy.

It's simple enough to remember that you recently disconnected the floppy drive cable to get at the memory sockets, so that if the drive light stays on and the floppy does not respond you know what to look for. In such a case the fault is almost always a data connector replaced either the wrong way round or with some pins not making contact. If the drive light does not come on at all, the fault is likely to be that you did not replace the power connector.

What is more difficult to recall, for example, is the cause of a lockup, with no key having any effect. This is particularly awkward if you have been typing fast, because you may have touched some key combination that you were not aware of. Usually this does no more than bring up a menu, but there are times when it causes a lockup — so much depends on the combination of hardware and software that you are using that no hard and fast rules can be given.

One comfort is that if what happened was because of a key that you pressed, then it is almost certainly a software fault, and it should be easier to deal with than some types of hardware faults. The other side of the coin is that a software fault is likely to cause loss of data if you have not saved your data recently. On the other hand, the experience is likely to make you more aware of the value of keeping backups.

Some software lockups are impossible to trace or to reproduce. These occur when you have been juggling with several programs, inserting and removing data and generally trying to do something awkward. All you can do is to try to remember to keep making backups so that when the crash happens you can be reassured that very little of your data will be lost.

Rebooting

A software fault usually leaves you with no control over the software, so that unless control returns (as it sometimes does) your only remedy is to reboot. Some machines can use a Reset button, others require you to switch off and then on again. If you have to switch off, leave a few minutes before you switch on again, because rapid switching on again can sometimes cause problems (in the power supply) that are much worse than the one that caused the fault. Incidentally, that was the cause of the only hardware fault I have suffered in the last fifteen years.

If the machine reboots normally, this confirms that the fault was due to software, and it might be helpful to find if you can reproduce the problem. Chances are that you can't, and you will simply have to note the incident so that you know to look out for it happening again.

Some types of fault will cause the machine to reboot on its own. These are rare and are usually due to software, but they are a hazard if you lose data. Once again, saving files at intervals and keeping backups are your main defence, because it is unusual to be able to fix this type of software fault for yourself.

Sometimes, rebooting will cause the CMOS RAM screen to appear. This is, strictly speaking, not a fault but a reminder that something needs to be changed, and some motherboards enter new data automatically, displaying the screen simply as a notification. The CMOS RAM contains details of drives and memory, and modern machines have several additional 'pages' of data relating to more advanced settings, such as to determine whether or not the floppy should be checked on booting up, or whether part of the memory should be set aside for a copy of the BIOS codes.

The first page of CMOS RAM will appear if you have made any major change, such as adding memory, adding or replacing a hard drive, or adding another floppy drive. In many cases, you will see the changes made for you, and you need only press the keys that save the new data and exit from CMOS RAM. On older machines you may have to enter information, and this is particularly important if you have added or changed a hard drive, when you need to enter a set of figures relating to the new drive.

Software crashes can sometimes have bizarre effects that leave other problems in place even after rebooting. For example, I had a lockup once that put the system clock forward by one century (to 2097). This in turn made it impossible to run two programs which from then on stopped with a memory violation error message. Restoring the correct year put everything back to normal.

Troubleshooting your PC

Keeping backups

The possibility of a fault, whether software or hardware, emphasises the importance of keeping backups of all your vital data. Apart from anything else, there will be a day when the hard drive will either not start, or will not provide the programs that allow the computer to boot up normally. This might not happen in all the years that you use your computer, and many owners who buy a new machine every five years or sooner will probably never experience a hard drive failure.

There is always a 'Friday drive', however, and yours might be the one that fails prematurely. You might be using a second-hand machine that was left running 24 hours per day — a good indication of this is that the monitor of such a machine usually suffers, and machines that have had such a hard life are offered for sale with a new or reconditioned monitor.

Whatever the fault, the loss of everything that was on a hard drive is something that you might have to face, and not necessarily because of a failure. Theft is another way of losing all the contents of a hard drive, and though you can insure a computer against theft (and remember that it costs more to insure a £2,000 computer than a £14,000 car) you cannot insure your data files which might represent years of hard work.

Any backup system has to represent value for money. After all, it might **never** be needed (just as it's **never** you who wins the lottery). A lot of backup systems are sold with the idea that you back up everything on a hard drive, which can mean buying a backup system that has the same capacity as your hard drive.

This is not realistic for several reasons. One is that your hard drive is probably not full, particularly if you are using a fairly new machine that, typically, uses a hard drive of 2

Gbyte or more. Another is that a lot of the space in your hard drive is taken up with programs that were loaded in from CD-ROM. Even if the computer had these programs pre-loaded, the supplier will have enclosed the CD-ROMs in the package. It's pointless to make a backup of material that is on CD-ROM, because few backups are as reliable a form of storage as the CD-ROM itself.

- You could object on the grounds that some programs, such as Word, can be configured so much to your own requirements that the program you have is not like the one that you loaded from CD-ROM. Fair enough, but the differences have not required great skill, and you are guarding against a fault that is not a serious risk, not on the same level as crossing a street.

- Any form of backup that you use should be able to back up the Windows Registry files. See Chapter 6 for details.

If you keep all your source discs in a safe place, failure of a hard drive is not much more than an inconvenience as far as programs are concerned, provided that you can replace Windows. When a new hard drive is installed, it might have MS-DOS preloaded, and you should be able to install Windows. If not, it is not difficult to load in MS-DOS, and its not a disaster if you have to get a CD-ROM that will install Windows completely from scratch on a newly formatted hard drive.

The files on the hard drive that are truly irreplaceable are your own data files, the ones you create with your word processor, spreadsheet, database, accounts program and so on. These should be backed up at regular intervals, and the backups kept where they are safe. If you run a small business, for example you might want to keep these backups at the bank, particularly when you go on holiday.

Troubleshooting your PC

Because your data files probably require less storage space than your program files, you can often backup quite simply by copying the files to floppies. Quite commonly, only a few files are used in the course of a week, so only these need to be backed up — you will already have backups of files that you no longer work on each day. Some programs, such as Intuit's *Quicken* accounts program, provide for making backups automatically. Other programs provide a macro system that can be used to ensure automatic backing up on floppy.

When the amount of data becomes too large for a reasonable amount of floppies, there is a danger that it will fall into disuse. If, for example, you have to juggle with 30 floppy discs each Friday, you are less likely to have much appetite for backups. This is where more advanced backup methods come in.

Microsoft Backup is part of Windows 95, and it can be used with floppies. Unlike a straight copy, however, Backup uses data compression so that the equivalent of 4 Mbyte or more of data can be fitted on one floppy. This alone is often enough to make backup simpler.

The ultimate is some form of specialised backup drive. At one time this was provided only by a tape cartridge, and modern tape cartridge systems are used in some low-cost (under £100) drives. Capacity figures range from 350 Mbyte to more than 2 Gbyte. A more modern tape system is DAT (digital audio tape) which provides large capacity on 8 mm tape cassettes that resemble the camcorder type.

There are other options. Removable hard drive systems use a casing that connects to the computer, often using a parallel port. A hard drive cartridge plugs into this case, and you can copy data to the drive, using compression if necessary. When you have backed up in this way, the cartridge can be unplugged so that you can store the data safely.

Yet another backup option is the creation of CDs. Drives can now be bought that will write a CD once and once only, but these are now being superseded by read/write CD drives. With the blank discs costing in the region of £3 the cost of the drive is soon recovered as compared to tape drives, whose cartridges are, by comparison, very expensive.

- One point to note is that Microsoft Backup currently works with only a limited number of tape drives of the older type. If you use anything other than these drives you will need to use other software. This may be supplied with the drive, but some software has to be bought separately.

If you have a video recorder, this can be used for backup, with a capacity of around 1.5 Gbyte on a 180-minute tape. You need an interface board that will plug into the computer and connect to the video recorder, along with software (you cannot use Microsoft Backup). The advantage of this method is that it requires only a small outlay if you already have the video recorder, and it uses cheap and readily obtainable tapes.

Another form of backup is useful as a last resort. If every document you have generated is printed and the paper is kept in a safe place, this can be read into the computer by using a scanner. It isn't a form of backup that you would want to use unless you had to, but it's useful to remember that data is not completely destroyed while any paper copies exist.

Describing the fault

Describing a fault to someone else, such as the listener on a Help line, can often be quite difficult. Do not try to make a description that forms a diagnosis. For example, don't describe a noise as coming from the hard drive unless you can be really certain about it. As far as you are concerned, the noise came from inside the box. If you sound as if you

know a lot about the computer, any help that you get might
be couched in expert's language and possibly not of much
use to you (like some error messages).

Any description of a fault needs some accompaniment. For a
hardware fault you should note odd noises, screen messages
(if the screen becomes active), and any other effects like
flashing indicator lamps. For a software fault you could note
what software was running (which might be several
programs if you were using Windows), what hardware is
installed, and, if possible, what keys you pressed just before
the fault arose. The content of any screen messages is also
useful.

Help text

There is a file named hardware.txt, which is located in the
C:\windows folder. If you encounter hardware problems you
should print and read this file, which contains many hints on
problems that arise with some specific makes of hardware,
particularly laptop machines. The headings used in this file
are listed below so that you can see if the contents might be
useful to you.

IBM Thinkpad	IBM Thinkpad Dock	Micron M5-PI
Micron P90/100	NEC Versa M	AT&T Globalyst
Winbook XP	HP Omnibook 600C	DEC Hi Note Ultra
Acer Acernotes	Compaq Aero	DEC Venturis Audio card
Media Vision Audio card	Zenith Noteflex 486DX	Megahertz Em1144T
Digital Venturis	Mozart sound card	Micronics motherboard

Toshiba models	Sanyo 3-D CD-ROM	Micron PowerServer
Scanners	Modems	Tape drives
Zip drives		

Help lines

If a software fault occurs that can be pinpointed to a program, you may be able to get help from the manufacturer through a help line. That's the official answer, but few who have used a help line have much faith in them for such reasons as long waiting periods, being passed from one helper to another, and so on. Nevertheless that's the bottom line as far as software errors go. Pinpointing the program that caused a shut-down is easier, because you will usually get a message about the fault. You should click the button that provides details of the fault, and write down what you see, even if it makes very little sense to you.

When you contact a Help line you will certainly be asked what you did just before the fault developed. You may also be asked for the message that appeared in the fault panel. All of this might be a well-known fault, so that you get a fairly swift reply. On the other hand, you might be asked to run a diagnostic program and send in the disc that it produces.

Help yourself

The remainder of this book is devoted to do-it-yourself work. Some of this might call for opening the casing of the PC, and though all accessible points inside the main casing are at harmlessly low voltage levels, you can still do damage (to the PC, not yourself) by touching parts aimlessly. You should **never** attempt to open a monitor or a printer, since both of these present hazards that need to be tackled by a professional or other experienced person. Some important points to remember are:

Troubleshooting your PC

- Remember basic electrical safety.

- Always switch off and disconnect the mains cable if you intend to open the casing of the computer.

- Never allow children to open electrical equipment or to touch the inside of any computer equipment.

- Never work alone.

- Always make a note of what you intend to do and in what order.

- Always make a note of the position of connectors and any other items that you have to disconnect or shift.

2 Drive faults

Drive faults are particularly to be feared, because they threaten the files that are more valuable than the computer itself. Even a fault in the floppy drive has to be taken seriously because without a working floppy drive you cannot make backups unless you have another type of backup drive. The most dreaded fault is one that affects the hard drive, and some large computers deal with this by using the RAID system, meaning redundant array of individual drives. This means that several hard drives, typically 5 to 10, are used, with every piece of data duplicated and spread over the drives. In this way, failure of one drive leaves the data intact, and the drive can be replaced without needing to shut the computer down.

At the risk of becoming a backup-bore, I have to repeat that a hard drive failure is bad news at any time, but if you do not have backups it is a total disaster. The drive may house all your work, your tax return data, accounts; everything that you depend on for your living. If you have backups you could read the backups into another computer and carry on. If you have no backups you may have no business, and no income.

Total failure

One classic symptom of a hard drive failure is that the drive motor simply does not start when you switch on the computer. The lights all come on in the usual way, but instead of the familiar whine of the drive motor running up to speed, you hear nothing except the computer fan(s) working. Needless to say, the machine does not boot, and there may be a message on the screen to the effect that the *System tracks* cannot be read.

This is serious, but there may be some hope. The cause, if the drive is an old one, is often a sticky drive motor. The motor of a hard drive is not powerful, and it needs only the smallest amount of friction to develop to prevent it from starting, though it will run perfectly if it starts.

The only long-term remedy is to replace the hard drive, but there are some desperate measures that you can take to get the drive going. I am assuming that the drive is a fairly old one, because it is most unlikely that this would happen to a new, or fairly new, drive. If your hard drive is fairly new, do not attempt this rescue method because it will invalidate any guarantee that still exists.

Switch the machine off, and prepare whatever you need to make any backups that you have not yet made. Open the casing and locate the hard drive — it's a flat casing with two sets of cables. This will be located close to the other drives, though in tower cases it is often located high in the rear portion of the PC, opposite the other drives.

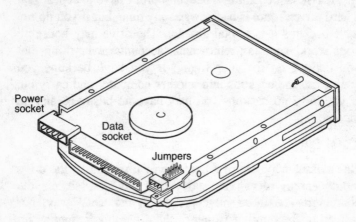

Put one hand on the casing, making sure that you are not touching anything else. Now switch the computer on and at the same time, tap the drive with your finger. With luck, you will hear the drive start and come up to full speed, and the computer will boot.

This works for some types of drives, but not for others, and it really is a last-ditch measure. If the machine starts, you should make any backups you need, and note the type of hard drive. You should then order a new drive. You might want to upgrade the drive, since hard drives are now very cheap compared to their prices a few years ago. If you do so, check that a newer drive will work in your machine — any machine that is old enough to experience a total hard drive failure may not be able to use modern drives in a straightforward way. In particular, an older machine may not be able to use a drive of more than 512 Mbyte.

Bad track faults

Total hard drive failure is often totally a hardware fault, but it can be due to corruption of the software in the machine if the modern alterable ROM chips are used or if the ROM codes are copied to RAM when the machine is switched on. Another hardware possibility is that the magnetic platters in the drive are damaged, but the drive motor is working. In this case, you will hear the drive working, but the machine does not boot up, and you get the message about not reading system tracks.

Before engaging panic mode, just check to see if there is a floppy in its drive. Many machines, at boot time, check for a floppy in the drive, and attempt to boot up from that floppy. If the floppy does not hold MS-DOS tracks (the system tracks), and error message appears and the system waits for you to do something. What you should do is to remove the floppy and then press the Return key, when you should see the machine boot from the hard drive.

• Some machines allow you to make CMOS RAM settings that will ignore the presence of a floppy, always booting from the hard drive. This is useful, but you will need to be able to alter these settings if you have a hard drive failure and need to be able to boot from a floppy.

Assuming that the cause of the problem is not a floppy in the drive, what now? This type of problem is less serious than it looks, and you can even get some more life from the drive, though if it is more than five years old it would be wise to look for a new drive soon. What has happened is that there is some damage to the part of the drive that holds codes that are used at boot time. If you can use the *ScanDisk* program on the drive, it can be 'repaired'. The repair consists of finding the defective portions, re-locating data from them, and shutting off the defective tracks on the drive. These tracks will not be used again, so that the drive becomes useable again, though you might have lost some data — that's why you keep backups.

Recovery is easy enough, but not if your computer experience has been only using Windows. Windows cannot be run from a totally crippled hard drive, and it cannot be run from a floppy. You can, however, run MS-DOS from a floppy, and that's how the repairs are done. At some stage, you should have prepared a Startup disc — see Appendix A if you are in doubt. This disc contains MS-DOS and several auxiliary programs that can be used for running repairs, among them ScanDisk.

Here's what you are advised:

Put the Startup disc in the floppy drive and switch on the PC. You should hear the floppy spin and messages on the screen will show that MS-DOS is loading. You need to ignore any message you get that reads *Starting Windows 95*. Eventually, the screen will show the A:\ which indicates that MS-DOS is loaded and the current drive is the floppy. You can then type ScanDisk C:\ to check the hard drive and repair any faults.

That's the official version, and it may work perfectly on your computer. However in 1997 Microsoft started to issue a

16

revised version of Windows 95 that makes better use of the hard drive space. This version is referred to as FAT32 or OSR2. The version of ScanDisk that is currently placed on a Startup disc will **not** run with this system, and you get the error message:

C:\ is not a valid name for a Drivespace volume file

instead of the repairs to the hard drive. This makes any recovery much more difficult. By the time you read this, it's likely that this will have been remedied, but you should check as soon as possible — it's not something that you want to find out when you have a boot failure and want to get going again. Your machine may be one that was bought in the time between introducing OSR2 and sorting out the ScanDisk program.

To test the floppy, start up the computer in DOS (using the menu that appears when you press the F8 key while booting up), or opt to restart in DOS when you shut down. When in DOS, insert the Startup disc into the floppy drive, and type:

A:\ (press Return)

With A:\ now appearing on screen, type the ScanDisk command in the form:

Scandisk C:\

and if this runs the ScanDisk program in the normal way then your Startup disc can be relied on.

Even if you cannot run ScanDisk from the floppy, you may be able to reach the data in the folders on the hard drive. Using MS-DOS you need to know the path to a folder, so that if your data is in the folder called:

C:\Data\Documents\Mywork

You can reach this folder by using the command:

CD C:\Data\Documents\Mywork

17

and pressing the Return key. When the folder name is acknowledged on screen, you can use the DIR command to see the folder contents, and the COPY command to copy the files to a floppy (if they will fit). The format of command to copy all files in a folder to a floppy is:

COPY *.* A:\

and if the files take up too much space you will be notified. You can use DIR A:\ to find how many files have been copied, and copy the others individually onto another floppy.

In addition, you might be able to start Windows by changing to the C:\windows folder and issuing the command:

Win (press Return key)

If this starts Windows, you can then use the version of ScanDisk that is part of the System Tools. This will certainly work with the OSR2 type of hard drive configuration. See later for details of Windows ScanDisk.

Restoring system tracks

Failure to boot from the hard drive usually means that something has happened to the system tracks, the portions of the hard drive that hold the MS-DOS boot-up files. If you can boot up from the Startup floppy you can restore these files by using MS-DOS commands. The procedure is:

1   With A:\ showing on the screen, type:

path = C:\windows\command   (press Return)

2   Type the command for replacing the files:

SYS A: C: (press Return)

Note that the spaces are **very** important. When the SYS command has completed its action, you should see *a System Transferred* notice on your screen.

- From all this you can see that another useful part of your backup system should be a good book on MS-DOS, so that you have a full list of commands and the way in which each command is used.

Hard drive maintenance

Whatever version of Windows 95 you have, the version of Scandisk that is used **from within Windows** is capable of working with the hard drive. You should run this utility at intervals to ensure that you catch any problems before they become serious. It's normal to find fragments of files sometimes, and this is not a worry — they are almost always the result of deleting files, or shutting down the computer while a file is in use.

What would be a worry is if a surface scan of the hard drive came up with defective sectors. This does not mean that the drive cannot be used, because Scandisk will ensure that these sectors will not be used again. The worry is that the drive is starting to deteriorate, and if you get the message about defective sectors or tracks twice in successive runs of Scandisk, or you get more than two reports in a year, it's probably time to get a new hard drive. You should also be more than usually careful about keeping backups.

To run Scandisk from Windows 95:

1   Click the Start button, and go through Programs — Accessories — System Tools.

2   Click on ScanDisk in this set, and follow the instructions on screen.

Another way to this is to use Windows Explorer. Click the *My Computer* title in the folders section and click the C:\ hard drive name in the files section. Now click File — Properties, and when the panel appears, click *Tools*. The topmost item is *Error-checking Status*, and you should click on the *Check Now* button to start ScanDisk running.

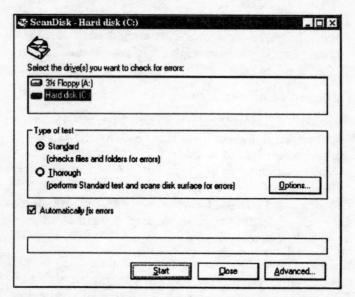

You have the options of a quick check of files and folders, or a thorough surface scan that checks the drive condition as well. Use the surface scan once a month or so, with the *automatically fix* option turned on, and look for any messages that appear concerning errors that have been found and fixed.

ScanDisk should always be run if you have had faults appearing in any other software, causing lockups or reboots. A fault in a data file can be a cause of such problems, particularly for large programs like Word, but if you have a backup of the file that can be used without problems, the corrupted version can be replaced after running ScanDisk.

- ScanDisk will, using the default options, make a file from any fragments that it can rescue from a corrupted file. These rescued files will appear on the C:\ folder typically as file0001.chk, each carrying a different number. You can read the smaller files using Notepad, and the larger ones using WordPad, but if these have been program files there will be nothing useful that you can get from them. If these are data files you can save the data into another file.

- Your machine may run ScanDisk automatically after booting if, on the previous run, the computer was switched off before leaving Windows.

CMOS-RAM screen

The CMOS-RAM screen reveals the data that is stored in this small part of memory, and it usually appears only if you have pressed the appropriate key(s) at boot time. The key or keys that must be used depends on the machine and the ROM manufacturer, and you will have to find this from the manual or from messages that appear on the screen while the computer is booting.

- One common starting key is the Del key, used just before MS-DOS is loaded; but it is just as common to use key combinations, like Ctrl–Alt–S. This is something you need to find for yourself, and note.

STANDARD CMOS SETUP

```
Date: (mm:dd:yy): Thu, Aug 28 1977
Time: (hh:mm:ss): 16 : 36 : 19

HARD DISKS          TYPE  SIZE  CYLS HEAD PRECOMP  LANDZ  SECTOR  MODE
Primary Master     :User  2568  622   128     0      4981    63     LBA
Primary Slave      :None    0     0     0      0        0      0     ____
Secondary Master   :Auto    0     0     0      0        0      0     AUTO
Secondary Slave    :None    0     0     0      0        0      0     ____

Drive A: 1.44M, 3.5 in.
Drive B: None
Floppy 3 Mode Support: Disabled    | Base Memory:         640K
                                   | Extended Memory:    31744K
Video: EGA/VGA                     | Other Memory:        384K
Halt On : All Errors               | Total Memory:       32768K
```

On older machines, the CMOS-RAM display is usually quite modest, but the amount of information has increased over

21

the last few years, so that the data can fill several screens, and is divided into pages.

- Unless you are fairly expert, the first of the CMOS-RAM pages is the only one whose settings you should work on, unless you have been advised by the manufacturer to alter other settings. There are settings on other pages that set aside memory for actions like copying ROM contents, and if these have not been set by the computer manufacturer you should take advice before altering them.

The CMOS-RAM screen may appear without any keys having been pressed, and this usually indicates that you have just changed something, like adding memory or a hard drive. If the CMOS screen appears when you have not been making such changes, then it indicates that something has gone wrong, and you should read the screen information carefully. It helps greatly if you know the normal content of this first page of CMOS-RAM, and noting this should be a priority when you acquire a new computer. Some manuals even provide a blank form on which you can note the settings.

It's important to note any changes that you make in the CMOS-RAM. Changes in the first page usually reflect changes in hardware, but if you have been altering other settings this need not have any connections with hardware.

If you get the CMOS-RAM window appearing when you boot, and you have not changed hardware, then the screen appearance has been triggered by some other change, and if you have a note of what you changed and what the previous value was you can restore settings if this is required.

Avoiding trouble

Avoiding trouble is better than curing it, and a lot of trouble relating to drives can be avoided by maintenance. This, for most users, means running ScanDisk at intervals. This action has already been described, and you will be reminded, when you use File — Properties on the hard drive, of the time that has elapsed since you last ran ScanDisk on your hard drive.

Chapter 8 deals with how to replace a hard drive or add a second hard drive.

Drive performance

On machines manufactured since early 1997, the version of Windows 95 has been labelled 4.00.950b. To check this, select *My Computer* in Windows Explorer and click the File — Properties item. If your computer was new at any time later than June 1997 it is almost certain that this version will be in use. This is the OSR2 version, see earlier, and you can confirm this by looking at the Properties panel for the hard drive, which should carry the label *FAT32*. This late version of Windows 95 is very similar in important respects to Windows 98.

On your OSR2 computer, you can speed up access to the hard drive and to the CD-ROM drive by enabling DMA (direct memory access). This is done as follows:

1   Start Control Panel, and click in succession *System*, *Device Manager* and *Disk Drives*.

2   The *Disk Drives* section should show both the floppy and the hard drive, with the hard drive usually identified as IDE, possibly with Type 46.

3   Click this line, and then click on the Properties button. Click Settings, and look for a box labelled DMA. PIX dmabox ✔

4   If this is not ticked, click on it. When you leave the Settings panel you will be asked to reboot the computer.

5   When your computer is running again, go back to the Device Manager and this time find your CD-ROM name.

6   Click the Properties — Settings and locate the DMA box. Click this to place a tick in the box, and carry on to the reboot stage as before.

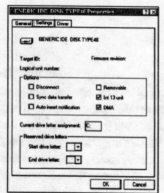
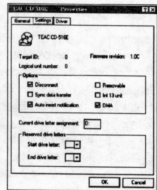

By ensuring that these DMA boxes are ticked, you can speed up these actions of loading and saving, and since these are critical to overall speed of the computer, you should gain in better performance. These options are not available in earlier versions of Windows.

3 Keyboard, mouse, loudspeakers

The keyboard and the mouse can be potent sources of trouble, particularly on an older PC. Troubleshooting and maintenance tips follow, but you can help yourself by ensuring that:

1   The keyboard is always covered when it is not in use, and,

2   the mouse is used on a clean surface so that it does not pick up dust.

All new keyboards come with a cover, and because the pattern of the PC keyboard is fixed, apart from types like the Microsoft Natural Keyboard or the Dvorak keyboards, any cover should be suitable, and you can buy replacements if your cover is missing. If you use a mouse mat, cover it with a piece of cloth when the mouse is not in use, so that dust does not accumulate on the mat.

• Some care over these items will be repaid by fewer problems, particularly with the mouse.

Both keyboard and mouse can suffer software faults as well as hardware faults. Faults that develop during use of the computer are usually hardware faults, but if you are setting up a new machine you need to ensure that the driver software will be loaded. This is done by entries into the files called autoexec.bat and config.sys.

These files are located in the C:\ folder, and you can read them and edit them using Windows Notepad. The autoexec.bat file should contain a line such as:

LH KEYB UK

which will load the KEYB file that is part of the keyboard driver, and ensure that it is configured for UK use. The mouse driver is supplied from Windows.

Troubleshooting your PC

- If you start in MS-DOS you are likely to see a different version of the autoexec.bat file that has been modified by Windows, but this should not affect your KEYB line.

You can use the Windows Control Panel to check the drivers that are in use. Double-click on System, and then:

1 Click *Device Manager*, then *Keyboard*.

2 Select the keyboard type, which is usually 102-key.

3 Use the *Properties* tab to look at *Device Status*. This should show a message to the effect that the device is working normally.

4 Look also at *Resources*. If the report on this panel is *No conflicts* then you should have no software problems with the keyboard.

Reports of conflicts or of the device not working can often be resolved by using one of the trouble-shooter routines from the Windows 95 Help menu. Problems are likely to arise if you have swapped keyboards or tried to install another driver.

The mouse will **not** appear on the *Device Manager* set unless there is a separate mouse port in use. The fashions in mouse connection change at intervals, and your mouse may be connected through a PS/2 mouse port, in which case there should be a Device Manager setting. If, as is quite common, the mouse is one that plugs into a serial port, you can check only that this port is working, not for the action of anything connected to it.

- You will not find any reference to the mouse in the config.sys or autoexec.bat files unless you need to use the mouse for MS-DOS programs. If you use the mouse only for Windows programs, the driver is contained within Windows.

Key problems

A sticking key on a keyboard can cause a fault that looks very much more serious than it really is. The machine will not boot correctly, and you will see a message that displays a code number (the code for that key). Look for the telltale sign or a key that is squint, and you will have solved the problem.

- Another type of problem is the key that will not make good contact. The temptation is to thump it, which ensure that the trouble becomes steadily worse. The only long-term solution is to replace the keyboard.

Any mechanical work on a keyboard needs watchmakers' skills. If you have nothing to lose you might be able to sort out a sticky key or one that makes poor contact, but you should be resigned to buying a new keyboard if your efforts meet without success. Keyboards are often of the membrane type and these are not easily sorted out (nor are they intended to be). The better type of keyboard that uses a superior form of switch is easier to work on, but this is no guarantee that you can improve things.

- Whatever you do, avoid spraying silicone lubricants, such as the well-known WD40, on to your keyboard. This is more likely to get between contacts and ensure that electrical connection is never possible again. You should, in fact, avoid spraying anything on to plastic surfaces on the computer.

If the worst comes to the worst, choose a replacement keyboard with care. If you like a keyboard with a positive click action you may have to try out several types before you find one that suits you. Make absolutely certain that the connector is the same as is used on your computer.

Troubleshooting your PC

Spilled drinks

Spilled drinks are a serious hazard, because even if you can dry out the keyboard, the remnants of the drink will still cause trouble. Drinks that contain sugar will leave a sticky residue that can cause sticking, and all drinks are likely to leave remnants that will cause electrical short circuits between key contacts. These will cause the same problems as sticky keys.

- As an emergency measure, you can configure the CMOS RAM for *No keyboard*, so that the keyboard can be disconnected without causing error messages, and the mouse used alone. This is no comfort if you were about to enter a large amount of text, but it does at least give you some control over the computer until the keyboard can be replaced. Remember when you replace the keyboard to alter the CMOS-RAM to show that the keyboard is present.

Connectors

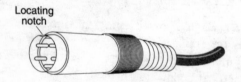

Locating notch

Keyboard connectors are another potential source of hardware trouble. These will be either the DIN type of plug and socket, illustrated, or the miniature PS/2 type, and they have no form of locking to prevent them from pulling out. The usual type of keyboard cable contains a curled section which is quite heavy, and if this dangles so that it is pulling on the connector then sooner or later the connector will come out. Make sure that this curled section is resting on the desk or otherwise supported.

28

Remember that if you move the computer, the keyboard connector has to be checked afterwards, as this is the one most likely to become detached. Always reinsert the connector carefully, because it should fit only one way round, and forcing it will bend the pins, ensuring that it will never fit again.

Lock switches

The lock switches of the keyboard are used to lock some action on and are labelled Num Lock, Caps Lock and Scroll Lock. All of these except the Caps Lock are remnants of older keyboard requirements, and there is no modern application for the Scroll Lock key.

The Num Lock is usually switched on by default, ensuring that the numerical keypad on the right hand side of the computer delivers numerals rather than the cursor-moving actions. You can toggle this action by pressing the Num Lock key, and you can change the default from the CMOS RAM settings (not on the first page but on a later one of the CMOS RAM display).

The Caps Lock will reverse the letter action, so that pressing a letter key gives the capital letter, and pressing the letter key along with Shift gives the lower-case letter. Some programs, such as Word 97, will detect unintended use of the Caps lock, and another useful tip is to use the *Accessibility* options of Windows 95. The *Key* options of *Accessibility* include one that provides sound when any of the lock keys is used, and this can be very useful if you often hit the Caps Lock by accident when you are typing fast.

- Do not use the FilterKeys option unless you really need it, because it slows down key action dramatically

Windows 95 keys

Some keyboards use the three added Windows 95 keys. Two of these are identical, placed next to the Alt and Alt Gr keys, and are labelled with the Microsoft flag. The other is to the left of the Ctrl key and is labelled with an icon of a page and arrow.

These keys provide alternative methods of obtaining menus that avoid clicking. The Microsoft flag keys will produce the Start menu, and this is particularly convenient if you opt to hide the Windows 95 taskbar, using Start — Settings — Taskbar — Auto hide. The other key produces the same menu that you get by using the right-hand mouse button. The contents of this menu will depend on where the pointer is placed at the time when you press the key.

Mouse problems

If your mouse has absolutely no effect, then the hardware reason may be that the connector has come loose. This is more likely when the PS/2 or DIN plug type of connector is used, because a serial connector can be locked into place. A loose connector on the mouse cable is unusual, because the cable is light and does not tend to drag on the connector, but you may have inadvertently pulled the cable.

The software reason for no mouse action is that no mouse driver has been loaded. This is unusual if you use only Windows, because the mouse driver is included in Windows. You might need to reinstall Windows to restore your driver, but if you are forced into this type of drastic action remember that any part of Windows that stores your settings will be replaced (such as Cardfile entries, phone numbers, etc.). If you use MS-DOS applications, you may find that the mouse action is missing because the MS-DOS application does not provide for a mouse, or because the Autoexec.bat file for MS-DOS does not load a mouse driver such as MOUSE.COM.

Windows 95 contains drivers for the common types of mouse, and also for some three-button mice such as the Logitech. Note that if you want to make use of the centre button on a Logitech mouse you should use the Logitech driver (Mouse Control Centre) that is supplied with the mouse. If your computer has a PS/2 mouse port but you are using a Logitech serial mouse you may have to use the *Device Manager* (in the System set from Control Panel) to change from *PS/2* to *Logitech serial mouse*.

If your computer uses a mouse from Genius or Mouse systems, you can use the standard Microsoft driver providing you do not use the third button. You can find driver updates in the \Drivers\Mouse folder of the Windows 95 CD-ROM.

Cleaning mouse rollers

The most common hardware mouse complaint is that the pointer on the screen does not follow the mouse movements correctly. The action may become sticky, which points to dirt on the mouse rollers. This dirt is picked up on the ball of the mouse and transferred to the internal rollers. There it will build up until the rollers jam intermittently, and the only remedy is to clean the rollers.

• You will often see advice about cleaning the ball. This is by itself often quite useless, because the ball does not usually cause much trouble, but you should clean it when you clean the rollers.

To clean the rollers and ball:

1 Turn the mouse over, and unscrew the ball cover by a quarter of a turn. Put your hand over the cover and flip the mouse over so that the cover and the ball fall into your hand. You can now see the rollers.

2 Turn the mouse upside down again, and wrap a small piece of clean cloth (an old handkerchief cut into small strips is ideal) round the end of a pair of tweezers.

3 Dip the cloth into a suitable cleaning solution — an ideal cleaner is spectacle lens cleaner, and this usually comes in a spray pack, making it easier to dampen the cloth.

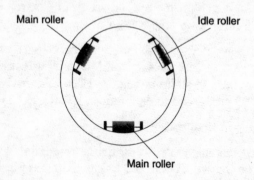

Main roller

Idle roller

Main roller

Squeeze any surplus moisture out so that the cloth is not dripping wet.

4   Rub the cloth sideways along a roller, pulling slightly so that the roller rotates. Keep doing this until the roller looks clean, and repeat on the other rollers.

5   Allow ten minutes to dry, in which time you can use a larger piece of cloth along with the same cleaning fluid to clean the ball. Allow this also to dry.

6   Put the ball back in place and close the retainer by a clockwise quarter turn.

Mouse response

The mouse response is controlled by Windows software, though some older varieties of mice had a small button that could be clicked to alter the response times. To alter mouse response, open Control Panel and double-click on *Mouse*.

1   The *Settings* panel will appear with its four tabs.

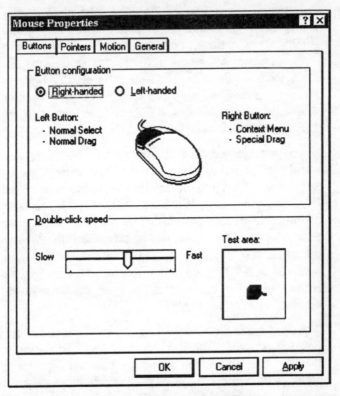

2 The first tab covers button use. You can set up the mouse for right-handed or left-handed use, but do not assume that if you are left-handed it is better to reverse the mouse buttons. Try it for yourself and see if you prefer it.

3 The other part of this panel controls the double-click speed, allowing you to move the slider until your favourite speed of double-clicking will operate the test item, a jack-in-the-box. You can click the *Apply* button to make a change and stay with the panel, or *OK* to make the change and return to Control Panel.

4   The second tab is marked *Pointers*. The main display
    shows the pointers that are currently in use for various
    Windows 95 actions. You can opt to use a *Scheme*,
    meaning a pre-set group of pointers, by clicking the
    arrowhead on this box. The default is usually *None* or
    Windows Standard, with the options of *3D Pointers*,
    Animated Hourglasses, *Windows Standard (Extra
    Large)* and *Windows Standard (Large)*.

5   If you are worried about the speed of your computer,
    avoid the 3D and animated effects because they require
    more work from the processor. The **Microsoft Plus!**
    Program, now part of Windows OSR2 upgrade, contains
    additional animated pointers. You can also select from
    three sizes for each individual pointer, using the *Browse*
    button. In this way, you can make up a scheme of your
    own, using the *Save As* button to preserve your scheme
    for posterity. You can also, if you want, delete an added
    scheme.

6   The third tab is for *Motion*. You can set the speed at any
    position between *Slow* and *Fast*, and the *Fast* setting is
    usually preferable for many users. You can also opt to
    show pointer trails (mouse-tails) which are useful for
    portable machines with LCD screens (making the
    pointer movement visible), but not needed on a desktop
    with a cathode-ray tube monitor. The duration of trails
    can also be set. Try it for yourself to see if you like a
    pointer that leaves a trail.

7   The last tab is *General*, and is used only when you need
    to change the type of mouse.

You should take some time over the settings of such items as
double-click speed, because if the settings match your
normal use of the mouse you will be able to work faster
because you will seldom need to repeat a double-click
action.

Loudspeakers

Loudspeakers are inevitably a part of any multimedia setup, and are usually of the active type, meaning that one loudspeaker casing (the master) contains a pair of amplifiers for the two. This is because the sound card on the computer can provide only a fairly weak signal, well below the power that is needed for realistic sound effects and music.

Active loudspeakers need a mains connection, and have some form of mains switch such as a button on the back or front of the master loudspeaker. Obviously, unless this is switched on there can be no output from the loudspeakers. The signal connection from the sound card uses a miniature jack plug type of connector, and this must be plugged into the correct socket on the sound card — there are usually three identical sockets, with the other two being used for a microphone input and a line input. The microphone input is very sensitive, and must not be used for anything other than a microphone. The line input can be used for inputs from record players, tape recorders, music keyboards, etc. A port connector may also be fitted for specialised purposes.

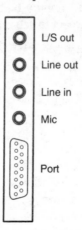

35

Troubleshooting your PC

The master loudspeaker will contain one or two volume controls, which should initially be set mid-way on their scale. If one volume control is used, there will be either a balance or a treble control fitted. If two volume controls are used, this allows you to control the speakers separately. It is less usual nowadays to fit a balance control or use separate volume controls because the software mixer (see later) can control stereo balance.

- One common fault is that the master loudspeaker works perfectly, but the other is mute, or works only intermittently. This is usually due to poor connections internally in the master unit, or stray wires contacting each other inside this unit.

These are hardware problems, but any loudspeaker system can be affected by software faults. These are either installation faults or control faults.

Unless a sound card is installed so that it is recognised each time the computer is switched on, it will not function. The initial installation of sound software should have attended to this, but you should check that the setup lines are present in the AUTOEXEC.BAT file. For a Soundblaster card, for example, you can expect to see lines such as:

SET MIDI=SYNTH:1 MAP:E MODE:0

SET SOUND=C:\PROGRA~1\CREATIVE\CTSND

SET BLASTER=A220 I5 D1 H5 P330 T6

and these indicate that the software has been installed correctly.

In addition to this, though, the sound system is controlled by the mixer software. This allows different inputs to be fed to the amplifiers, and it is possible that all inputs have been shut down, or that the enabled inputs are not inputs that you are using. To check this, use Start — Programs — Accessories — Multimedia and look for the title that relates to your sound board, such as Soundblaster. Clicking on this title should open another list of titles, and for the Soundblaster board you need to click on *Creative Mixer*.

- Many sound boards fitted to modern machines are either Soundblaster or closely compatible, so that the procedure should be much the same. You can also use the Windows mixer, see later.

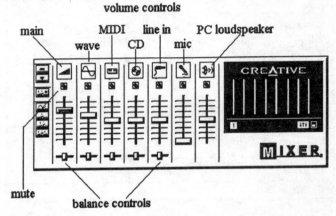

The Mixer panel contains one master volume control, and if this is at its minimum setting you will hear nothing from the loudspeakers. The small dots are mute switches, and clicking one of these will switch sound off or on, depending on the existing setting. You need also to look at the settings of the other volume controls. These are usually set to midway for all inputs, but if you see any set to zero, check that these are for inputs that you do not use. If the panel (as in the example) shows only icons for the inputs, placing the pointer on the button under the icon will produce an explanation for each icon.

You may find that another mixer is obtained when you click a loudspeaker icon in the bottom right hand corner of the screen. This is the Windows mixer, whose actions are identical to those of the Creative type. Clicking with the left-

Troubleshooting your PC

hand mouse button will produce a single volume control, the master control setting. Double-clicking with the left-hand mouse button will open another complete mixer set which is simpler to use than the Creative Mixer, and is illustrated here. On this type of mixer, the mute action is easier to distinguish, as it uses the familiar ticked box.

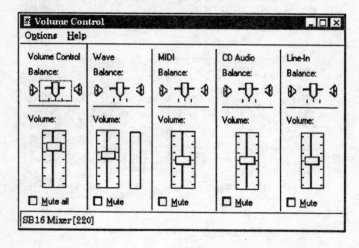

4 Monitor problems

Monitor hardware problems start with connectors and connections. The standard connector uses fifteen pins in three rows, and careless insertion can bend these pins. The data cable is particularly stiff and heavy, and the connector must be secured with its fixing bolts (do **not** screw these up tightly, they need be only finger-tight).

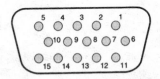

The pin use on the standard 15-pin D type connector for VGA is as follows:

1	Red out	2	Green out
3	Blue out	4	NC
5	Earth	6	Red earth
7	Green earth	8	Blue earth
9	No pin	10	Sync earth
11	NC	12	NC
13	Horizontal sync.	14	Vertical sync.
15	NC		

Note: NC = No connection, pin not used. Pin 9 is removed to act as a key.

Some older monitors use a 9-pin connector. These monitors may be used if they offer the correct signal connections, but you need to be absolutely certain that they will take the correct polarity and amplitude of signals. Older monitors with a 9-pin plug are usually monochrome, and though they can be connected up you need to know what you are doing.

Monitors that are suitable for the PC and which use a 9-pin connector are likely to use the following pin-out, and you can either connect the cable to a 15-pin plug or buy (or make up) a 9-to-15 adapter.

1	Red out	2	Green out
3	Blue out	4	Horizontal sync
5	Vertical sync	6	Red earth
7	Green earth	8	Blue earth
9	Sync earth		

- Note that if you are going to use a mono monitor, the Green output signal is normally used as the video signal.

The other connection between the monitor and the computer is likely to be the power line. The convention is to connect these two using the standard Euroconnector so that the monitor cannot be left switched on when the computer is switched off. This is very useful, but if you have other units that also need to be powered with the computer you should not attempt to connect several cables to the Euroconnector.

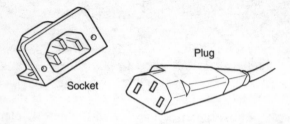

A better option is to use the connector at the computer end to supply a strip of sockets, with the units that are to be switched with the computer plugged into these sockets. This could include the monitor, loudspeakers of the active type, a scanner, an external modem; all items that take a low current. You can buy Euroconnectors suitable for this purpose from Tandy stores and other Electronics suppliers such as Maplin.

- You must observe the correct connection of live, neutral and earth pins, and if you have any doubt on this, get an electrician to make up the connections for you.

- The current rating of the main switch and Euroconnector on the computer is seldom stated, and you should not power the printer in this way, because printers can require comparatively large current levels at times. If you use the monitor along with an item such as loudspeakers or a scanner the current rating is unlikely to be exceeded.

Picture controls

The number and type of picture controls that are available for your monitor will depend on the design of the monitor, but brightness and contrast are always included. Modern monitors often add picture width and height and both vertical and horizontal position controls. A few monitors also offer tilt and degauss controls.

A degauss control will carry out a demagnetising action if there is colour corruption caused by internal parts of the tube becoming magnetised. The magnetisation is caused by placing loudspeakers too close to the screen, or by the difference in the Earth's magnetism when the monitor has been moved. If you see coloured shapes on what is intended to be a pure white screen, the degauss button can be pressed to clean this up. Many monitors are arranged to carry out a degauss action each time they are switched on. This automatic degaussing action is used on all colour TV receivers

Adjustments

Your monitor may have been perfectly adjusted as it was supplied. If the settings are unsatisfactory, you should adjust the brightness and contrast controls as follows:

1   If your monitor has a colour control, set this for a monochrome picture, otherwise use Control Panel — Display to change to a monochrome colour scheme. Display a picture, such as a piece of clipart, that covers the whole screen.

2   Set the contrast control to minimum.

3   Set the brightness control so that the black parts of the picture are acceptable (not grey).

4   Now increase contrast so that there is a good contrast between areas of different shading. The white should not be too glaring.

5   Make small adjustments to both brightness and contrast so that the picture looks pleasing.

6   Now restore colour, and make any last small adjustments to contrast and brightness.

Once contrast and brightness have been set you can make adjustments to width, height, and any controls that deal with picture shape (to correct bowing of vertical or horizontal lines).

Video cards

The conversion from digital signals inside the PC to video signals to the monitor is done in the video card, also known as the graphics card, graphics accelerator or video accelerator. The old VGA standard was for resolution of 640 dots horizontally by 480 dots vertically, using up to 16 colours on a picture. The lower number of resolved dots vertically is due to the shape of the picture which has a 4:3 ratio of horizontal to vertical size. Modern video cards will allow the use of both higher resolution and more colours if the monitor is capable, and these settings are known as SVGA, S for Super.

Dozens of suppliers have vied with each other to design and manufacture VGA and SVGA video cards. Some of the respected names in the video card business include ATI, Genoa, Matrox, Orchid, Paradise and Video Seven, and many well-known brands of computers will be found to include video cards by one of these suppliers. In addition, there are many less well-known suppliers who use these cards or cards by equally less well-known manufacturers. As long as these cards are genuinely compatible with the IBM standards then there should be no problems with software.

The trouble comes mainly if you want to use 'enhanced features'. You can find 640 x 480 resolution in 256 colours or even in 16 million colours (photo-real or 24-bit colour), 800 x 600 in 16 colours and even 1048 x 768 or more in four colours or sixteen colours. Some suppliers use the phrases *Colour, High colour* and *True colour*, with *True colour* referring to 24-bit or 32-bit colour coding.

There is a trade-off between resolution and number of colours, because increasing either requires more memory for video, and the amount built into the video card is limited, often to 1 Mbyte. Unless the card contains additional memory sockets that allow you to upgrade its memory the higher resolutions must inevitably be restricted to smaller numbers of colours at any given time (though the colours used on a screen can be picked from a large range). A few cards can plunder memory from the main RAM.

43

The number of colours corresponds to the number of digital bits used to code colour, and it does not imply that your monitor can display such a range of colour or your eye detect any differences between them. A memory of 2 Mbyte is adequate for most purposes unless you want to use more than 256 colours in high resolution.

Breaking away from the dominance of IBM in setting standards, a number of manufacturers of graphics cards have co-operated in setting a common standard called VESA (Video Extended Standards Association) so that producers of software can write drivers for the standard VESA resolutions. VESA supports the 800 x 600 16-colour mode, and this is the most important of the enhancements to VGA. Its resolution implies the use of square dots on the screen and is attainable by most monitors nowadays. The aim is that software producers can use a software driver which will suit any board produced by a VESA member to allow the use of all the VGA modes and the 'super-VGA' mode of 800 x 600. The 800 x 600 mode is also found in most of the VGA-type cards which are built into new computers as well as in add-on cards for older machines.

If you are tempted to use higher resolution graphics it is important to remember that you will need a monitor that is capable of displaying the higher resolution. This will be the type of monitor that is described as *non-interlaced*. You will also need a graphics card with at least 1 Mbyte of memory, possible up to 4 Mbyte. Having done this, you may find the displays of words and icons so small that you need to work very close to the screen. This is undesirable, so that high resolution should be used only along with larger screens, and for purposes like image editing and DTP work for which it is desirable. This in turn makes it very expensive.

- Remember that your ability to use high resolution is limited by the monitor. If you find that the higher resolution settings are greyed out when you use the Control Panel — Display settings, this indicates that these cannot be used. If your monitor type is not recognised by Windows, you can use one of the default standard types instead.

- When Windows 95 is set up, it uses a video driver on the basis of the type of video controller chip that is used in the video graphics board, such as S3, Cirrus, or ATI. In some cases, you can use Display Properties to find a more exact match in terms of make and model, and this will produce slightly better performance. Another video card option is speed. The time needed to put a display on the screen can limit the speed of the PC machine when you are using Windows so that several types of video cards have been developed which work faster at this task than others. Like Hi-fi, you can pay a lot of money for fairly modest increases in speed. Modern video cards all make use of the local bus connections (usually PCI) for increased speed. If you are interested in animated video displays, you must ensure that your video card is suitable and that its video software has been installed.

Some video cards offer the additional facility of connections to a TV or video recorder. This can be useful for presentations and for some games, but the connections are not quite as straightforward as it sounds, mainly because domestic TV receivers have resolution figures lower than 640 by 480. The instructions with the video card should be followed carefully, particularly warnings that you might need to turn off the monitor if it cannot use a 50 Hz refresh rate. Old TV receivers that do not feature a SCART connector or any other video input sockets are totally unsuitable, unless you also have a modulator that provides UHF output to the aerial socket of the TV.

Troubleshooting your PC

LCD screens

Portable, laptop and other miniature computers almost invariably use the LCD (liquid crystal display) type of screen which is used also on calculators and a host of other purposes. On this type of screen, the display consists of a fixed set of dots, each of which can be controlled separately so that it displays a colour.

This means that the screen layout is fixed. For example, if your LCD screen is 800×600, it cannot display a full-size picture if you set the video software to provide a 640×480 picture, and the effect of such a setting will be to show a smaller picture. This can be hard to come to terms with if you have been accustomed to using a conventional CRT monitor which will provide a full-screen picture for any resolution setting.

LCD screens are very vulnerable to pressure on the screen surface, which can cause damage to the internal connections. The screens that are fitted to laptop computers are more hardy than the types used on clocks and calculators, but you should try to avoid pressure on the screen surface. If a portion of the screen stops working, this usually indicates detached internal connections and there is nothing you can do about it.

Worse still, repairs to a portable computer are usually costly, and spares are often hard to obtain. Any sort of internal hardware work on a portable is definitely not for the inexperienced user and should be left in the hands of an expert. In fact, portable computers should be avoided like a plague unless you have absolutely no alternative.

Driver software

Assuming that the hardware is working correctly, problems with video displays can usually be traced to drivers. You are most unlikely to experience any problems with the standard

640 × 480 Microsoft driver that is included in Windows. Problems start to appear when you want to use the higher figures of resolution and/or colour numbers.

- When in doubt, always try a standard Microsoft driver if you are encountering problems. Manufacturers of video cards will supply drivers, but some of these can be of dubious quality.

Some of the problems relating to the monitor display software in higher-resolution modes can be resolved by clicking the *Graphics* button that appears in the *Performance* tab of the *System* item in Control Panel. The slider in this panel is usually set for maximum graphics acceleration, but if you suffer from odd effects such as portions of a graphics display remaining on screen after closing a menu box, try the slider in a lower position. The ultimate solution to such problems is to use the standard 640 × 480 resolution setting.

- If you encounter other monitor problems, look at the file called *display.txt* in the C:\windows folder. This contains information on known problems that affect some combinations of graphics boards and monitors, and is very helpful with both diagnosis and cure.

Power saving

Power saving software on a monitor can give the impression of a fault. All portable computers and many modern desktop machines now use power-saving to cut the electricity consumption of monitors, and the usual provision is to switch to low power after a set time, and even to switch off completely after a set time. On a portable machine, the blanking of the screen is not likely to be taken as a fault because the screen display is instantly restored when any key is pressed.

On a desktop machine, changing back from reduced power can also be fast, but changing back from a total switch-off takes longer because of the delay needed to heat up a cathode ray tube. This could give the impression of a fault, but as the display is restored within a minute it soon becomes obvious that the power-saving action is responsible.

These power-saving actions can be controlled from the Control Panel by double-clicking on the Display icon. Some type of video systems (such as ATI) place an icon on the Taskbar of Windows 95, and this icon can be double-clicked to alter the power (and other) display settings.

These power-saving actions are not available on older machines, and if you see the monitor display vanish it is more likely to be due to a screen-saver setting. If the display is not restored when you press a key, then suspect either the monitor or its driver software.

Size of print on the monitor

One problem that is very common is that the display is too small to read easily. This is particularly so if you use a resolution of 800 × 600 or higher on a 14 inch monitor, but even with a 17 inch screen, Windows icons and lettering can look uncomfortably small. Some portable machines should be supplied with a magnifying glass.

The standard portions of a window display are:

3-D Objects   Active Title Bar   Active Window Border

Application Background   Caption Buttons   Desktop

Icon   Icon Spacing (Horizontal)   Icon Spacing (Vertical)

Inactive Title Bar   Inactive Window Border   Menu

Message Bar   Palette Title   Scrollbar

Selected Items   Tooltips   Window

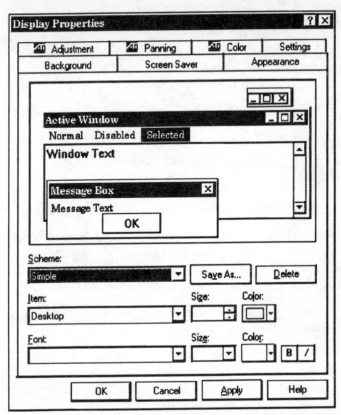

The solution is to alter the settings for each of these from the Control Panel, and save your alterations as a file that you can modify if needed. To do this:

1   Use the Control Panel — Display option and click the *Appearance* tab. This opens a panel that displays the appearance of a typical window.

2   You can click on any part of this display to see the name appear in the *Item* panel, along with entries in the *Size* and *Colour* boxes. This allows you to change the size, colour and font used for any part of a typical window display.

49

3   You can select from a range of preset displays. These
    are named, but the names are not necessarily a useful
    guide to their appearance. The current set of names is as
    follows, using abbreviation HC for High Contrast, L for
    Large and EL for Extra Large.

Brick   Desert   Eggplant   HC Black   HC Black (EL)

HC Black (L)   HC White   HC White (EL)

HC White (L)   Lilac   Lilac (L)   Maple

Marine (High colour)   Plum (High colour) (M)

Pumpkin (L)   Rainy Day   Red, White & Blue (VGA)

Rose   Rose (L)   Slate   Spruce   Stars & Stripes (VGA)

Storm (VGA)   Teal (VGA)   Wheat   Windows Standard

Windows Standard (EL)   Windows Standard (L)

• The larger sizes are useful when you are using the higher
  screen resolution figures.

4   You can create your own set of sizes and colours by
    selecting each portion of the display from the *Item* set,
    and clicking the arrowhead to bring up the size options.
    You can alter font and size of lettering, and size and
    spacing of icons. You can also change colours if
    appropriate.

5   Having created a display in this way, you can save it
    using a filename of your own by clicking the *Save As*
    button. If you use a name with no capital letters you can
    distinguish your own colour sets from these supplied
    with Windows.

• Remember that you can also change the fonts that are
  used for each portion of a Window display. The
  standard font is the MS Sans Serif, but you may prefer
  the appearance of some of the other fonts that you have
  on your hard drive.

- These colour schemes are used only for Windows programs, and will not appear in MS-DOS programs that you run using Windows 95.

5 Printer problems

A printer is by now such an essential part of a computer system that you tend to forget that it is seldom part of a computer package. Unlike the monitor, the printer is practically always bought separately, so that your choice of printer is important, since it may outlive several computers (in the sense that the computers are replaced by newer devices but the printer is not). Some printers may have a working life of ten years or more.

Output on paper is referred to as *hard copy*, and this hard copy is essential if the computer is to be of any use in business applications. For word processing uses, it's not enough just to have a printer, you need a printer with a high quality output whose characters are as clear as those of a first-class electric typewriter. For Desktop Publishing you will need a laser or inkjet type of printer. If you use CAD software to generate drawings with fine lines, a laser printer is essential because even the best inkjet printers produce rather grey lines on ordinary paper, not the glossy black of the laser printer. The differences are even more obvious under a magnifying glass.

Connections

Printer connectors have been standardised for some considerable time now. The power connector will use a standard UK 3-pin plug at one end and a Euroconnector at the other. A few printers have a permanent connection, but this is not so common because using a Euroconnector makes it easier to pack the printer without damaging the cable, and it also makes it easier to use longer cables.

For the data cable, virtually all printers use the Centronics type of parallel interface. The connector at the printer end is the Centronics 36-contact type, which relies on wedge-shaped strips of metal. This connector plug must be pushed home as far as it will go into the printer socket, and secured by the usual bolts. A loose data connector accounts for at least half of all problems with printers. At the computer end, the plug is a 25-pin D-type. This cannot be confused with a serial plug because it contains pins, not sockets.

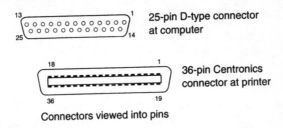

Connectors viewed into pins

Parallel printer leads are generally of up to 2 metres long, and many printer cables are only 1 m long. This restriction is due to the problems of interference that can arise in long cables. Long cables can cause erratic printer operation and incorrect characters appearing on paper. You can, if you need to, get around this restriction by using repeaters, amplifiers which restore the correct signals at the end of a long line, but few PC owners take this way out of a cable length problem.

Hardware problems

Mechanical problems with printers are surprisingly rare, despite the complex mechanism of many printers. My own record is one jammed sheet of paper and one jammed ribbon in the last ten years. One problem that can arise at times is paper jamming. Ordinary paper seldom causes any difficulties but envelopes and multi-part stationery can be troublesome, and some printers are very much better than others at handling such awkward materials.

Particular care is needed in handling sticky labels. These are normally mounted on a backing sheet, but if they become detached they can deposit their adhesive on rollers within the printer, causing problems until the rollers are removed and cleaned. If you want to use self-adhesive labels with a laser printer, make certain that the labels are laser-grade which can withstand the heat of the laser printer. The heat has nothing to do with the laser, just that the paper has to be heated to melt the (powder) toner into place.

A genuine mechanical fault will usually require the printer to be returned to the manufacturer or to a service agent. Before doing this, try the printer's self-test and test output routines. If a printer can produce a perfect copy of its test page (usually a sample of fonts) then a mechanical or electrical fault within the printer is unlikely to be the cause of the problem, which is more likely to arise from loose connectors or incorrect settings either at the printer or in the computer software. Remember, for example, that when you use the Windows printer manager the printer will not necessarily start printing immediately — it may wait until a queue forms or a 'print now' instruction is issued.

- Another problem is a software crash that has affected the printer driver. For example, if you find that printed paper suddenly uses different margins, perhaps with some lines printing over others, and with the printer paper looking nothing like the layout that appears on the screen, the cause is very often corruption of memory, and you should shut down both the computer and the printer and re-start after an interval.

The majority of printer problems concern failure to print what is expected, whether it is the £ sign on accounts statements or the graphics box shapes on a screen display. Using Windows, the printer will have been correctly set up for these actions, but this is not necessarily true if you want to print from a DOS application. The usual reason is that the printer has not been configured under DOS to use the correct character set. This will be PC-8 for laser printers, and the IBM #2 set for dot-matrix printers (most inkjet printers follow the Laserjet sets). Attending to this point solves some 95% of these DOS printing problems. In other respects, printers are remarkably reliable, particularly using Windows software.

If the main ON indicator fails to appear this can usually be traced to the mains switch of the printer switch being off or the power cable not correctly plugged in. Failing to print anything when the printer is clearly switched on is usually due to the printer being off line or the data cable incorrectly inserted — the data cable connector should be really firmly inserted and locked in place. Software can also cause what looks like printer errors, for example when the software is set for a line width that is greater than the page limits.

One important aspect of software concerns printer drivers. Most printers will perform adequately with text, but can sometimes provide very disappointing results with any kind of graphics work. This is often due to a poor printer driver, the software that matches the printer to the computer.

A few printer manufacturers will provide drivers for Windows and for each of the most popular non-Windows software packages, but if you have to use the driver that comes with the software, particularly if your printer is set for an emulation, you may encounter driver problems. Sometimes an upgrade is available, but if your printer is of an obscure make (and you do not always know what is an obscure make from a U.S. point of view) your only hope is that the printer manufacturer can provide a better set of drivers. Users of Windows who use only Windows programs are by far the most fortunate in this respect because they need only a single printer driver for Windows.

Types of printer

Printers that are used with the PC are mainly of three types. The most common nowadays is the inkjet, particularly for colour printing, but laser printers are still preferred for really clear black print. The impact dot-matrix type of printer is not so common now, but is still obtainable. More expensive types such as dye-sublimation printers are used for high-quality colour printing that gives photographic quality.

Ink-jet

The ink-jet printer operates by squirting tiny jets of ink at paper from a set of miniature syringes, and is a close second in quality to the laser printer for print and drawing quality. The bubble-jet technology, developed by Canon and Hewlett-Packard, has been widely adopted to make printers of remarkable quality and reliability at comparatively low prices.

This technology originated in the observation that a hot soldering iron laid on a hypodermic needle caused a drop of liquid to be ejected. The principle is to use a head consisting of fine jets (of a diameter narrower than a human hair) each provided with a miniature heater wire. Passing current through the heater for a jet will expel a tiny drop of ink, so that by driving these heater wires with the same form of signals as a dot-matrix impact printer, the ink can be deposited in the same character patterns.

A more recent development is the piezo-ink jet printer developed by Epson. The principle here is that part of the jet path is through a piezoelectric crystal (one that deforms when a voltage is applied to it), and when a voltage pulse is applied to the crystal it contracts, forcing ink from the jet. In principle, this can be a faster mechanism because there is no need to wait for the heating or cooling of an element, and it is possible that finer jets could be made. These printers are sold using the name *Stylus* and are very competitive in price.

All inkjets suffer from the compromises that have to be made in ink technology. The ink must be dry by the time the paper is moved, but wet enough to cling to the paper — no-one seems to have considered using the laser type of toner that can be melted into the paper. With ordinary paper, the ink spreads along the paper fibres, and it is this that causes narrow lines to look fuzzy, and black print to have a slightly grey appearance. Print quality can be greatly improved by using glossy paper, and this applies particularly to colour printing. This, however, raises printing costs enormously because the paper can cost as much as 10p per sheet.

Ink-jet printers are remarkably silent, considerably quieter than laser types (many of which have a noisy cooling fan). The speed of printing is not as high as that of the slowest laser type, but for many applications this is of little importance, and the ink-jet types have the advantage that they can also print in colour. The colour inkjet printers are sold at prices that are not substantially higher than the cost of black and white, though the cost of consumables is higher.

The main problems are of clogging of the jets. Some makes use a combined jet-head and ink cartridge, so that renewing ink means renewing jets. This almost eliminates clogging problems, but is an expensive solution, and many users resort to refilling ink reservoirs using kits that are widely advertised.

Laser printers

The ultimate in print quality is provided by the laser type of printer, which also includes variants such as LED bar printers and LCD-mask printers. These are fast and silent in action. The laser types are page printers, meaning that it is necessary to store a complete page of information in the memory of the printer in order to print the page. Fonts can be built-in, added by way of a cartridge (surprisingly expensive), or transmitted in bitmap form (downloaded) from the computer. If you print from Windows applications you can forget about built-in or cartridge fonts and use only the TrueType fonts of Windows.

- When elaborate graphics or downloaded fonts are used, this can require a large amount of memory within the printer. A typical amount is 2–3 Mbyte. Some LED bar types are not page printers, and can work line by line, requiring very little memory.

- The quoted speed of most laser printers refers to repeated copies of a single page and does not refer to normal printing, which can be considerably slower. All quoted printing speeds for printers of any kind tend to be optimistic.

Laser printers work on a principle called Xerography (Trade Mark of the Xerox Corporation) which was invented in the 1960s. The similarities between the laser printer and the Xerox photocopier are so close that the two products can be made in one assembly line. A page cannot be printed until the drum which is used to store the 'bit-image' of a page is fully 'printed' with electrical charges (the drum is usually 'printed' more than once to form a page, but the printing does not start until all the print-bits are assembled in the memory). The 'ink' is a dry powder which is melted into the paper by a heater.

Without going into further details of how the laser printer works, we can look at some restrictions. You need a ventilated space, because the printing process generates ozone, which is fairly toxic. The toner (ink) is comparatively harmless, but all fine powders are a risk to the lungs and also a risk of explosion. Toner stains on clothing or furniture can be removed using cold water, but vacuum cleaners are useless unless they are of a type (such as Nilfisk or Medivac) that can retain fine powders. Hot water will melt the toner, making it very difficult to remove.

The main consumables are the toner and the drum. The toner for most modern copiers is contained in a replaceable cartridge, avoiding the need to decant this very fine powder from one container to another.) Drum replacement will, on average, be needed after each 80,000 copies, and less major maintenance after every 20,000 copies. Some models use a separate developer powder (a magnetic powder) in addition to toner, and the developer will have to be replenished at some time when the toner is also exhausted. The Hewlett-Packard Laserjet machines use a cartridge which contains both the drum and the toner in one package, avoiding the need for separate renewal — the life is quoted at about 3500 sides at average print density of word-processed text, but this figure will be drastically reduced if you print a lot of dense graphics and fonts. Long-life cartridges are available for some models.

There are some types of printers which are classed as laser printers but which do not use a laser beam. These are LED-bar or LCD-mask types which use the same principles of light beams affecting a charged drum, but without the use of a laser beam scanning over the drum. These types are not page printers, and can work line by line, requiring very little memory.

Windows laser printers are a type that simplifies the printer and cuts costs by using the main memory of the computer and the main processor to prepare the data for the printer. They can be used only under Windows. Check before buying such a printer that it will operate under Windows 95 and Windows 98, and make certain that your computer uses enough memory to make this a viable option.

Impact dot-matrix

A dot matrix printer creates each character out of a set of dots, and when you look at the print closely, you can see the dot structure. The printer works by using the impact of a needle on an inked ribbon which in turn hits the paper.

The older type of dot matrix printer used a printhead that contained 9 wires or needles in a vertical line. This 9 pin, or

9 wire, printer type is still manufactured in large quantities, and some are sold at very high prices because of their particularly robust construction or high speed printing or both, but the later trend was to 24 pin printers.

By using two slightly staggered vertical rows of 12 pins each, these printers can print at a high speed and with excellent quality with none of the dotty appearance that has been associated with dot-matrix printers in the past. The noise level of such printers is usually higher than that of the 9 pin types, and ribbon life is shorter since so many more pins are striking the ribbon. Most 24 pin printers have built in fonts so that a range of different type styles can be obtained under DOS by operating switches on the printer itself, or under software control from your word processor if (and only if) it has a suitable printer driver. Used under Windows, the TrueType fonts will give good results.

- Each pin is, incidentally, of a smaller diameter than a human hair.

There is a huge range of manufacturers, but most printers are set up so as to emulate either the IBM range of Proprinters or the Epson. Some other emulations are not always satisfactory, because they can lead to a 24 pin printer being used to emulate a 9 pin type, so that the superior quality that the 24 pin type can provide for graphics use is not being utilised.

Reflecting older methods, most dot-matrix printers are equipped for continuous paper rolls or packs rather than using single sheets with a feeder. The printer settings must match the size of continuous paper that is used. Sheet-feeders are available for most models, but are an expensive extra.

- Colour dot-matrix printers are also obtainable, but the colour print quality is not up to the standard of inkjet machines, and the ribbons are costly.

Paper jams and staining

Paper jamming is one of the most common causes of print failure, but it need not happen on a well-maintained printer. The problem is confined to machines that use sheet feeders (inkjet and laser printers), and jamming of continuous paper feeders (tractor feed or pin feed) is very unusual.

One cause of paper jamming on laser or inkjet machines is curling paper. Paper should lie flat in the sheet-feeder, and not curl, but if you print a sheet on a laser printer and then immediately turn it over to print the other side it is almost certain to cause trouble. If you want to print both sides, print the odd-numbered sides first (most word processors will do this), and leave the paper to cool, then stack it under a weight to straighten it. The even pages can then be printed.

The other main cause of paper jamming is a sticky roller. This can usually be traced to printing on sticky labels, and is more often a problem with laser printers (because of the heating used to fuse the dry toner into the paper). Rollers are often made from spongy material, and if the roller can be removed easily it can be washed with soap and water and left to dry.

Paper staining on a laser printer is caused by a leak of toner. The toner lands on a roller so that it is transferred to each page that passes through the printer. The remedy is to clean the roller by washing it in **cold** water, clean toner from the inside of the printer, and change the toner cartridge.

- Watch for anything that could cause a printer to jam, such as a paper-clip falling onto a sheet that is about to be printed. Stop the printer immediately, because this type of jamming could cause damage, unlike a simple paper jam.

Troubleshooting your PC

Replenishing ribbons, ink, toner

Replenishment of consumable items is the main cost in running printers, and though the laser printer's cartridges look expensive, the cost per sheet printed can be less than that for an ink-jet. The impact dot-matrix type of printer is usually the most economical to run.

Ribbons

Ribbons for the older type of 9-pin dot matrix printer are comparatively cheap. The older Epson types in particular use a large ribbon cartridge, and the ribbon suffers very little mechanical wear, so that re-inking is quite easy and economical. The cartridge is opened carefully, and the ribbon smeared with the type of ink sold for rubber stamps. Do not let the ribbon escape from the cartridge because it is most unlikely you will ever get it back in place again. If a ribbon jams, scrap it.

Ribbons for 24-pin printers are usually in smaller cartridges that move with the print-head. These have a much harder life, are more expensive to replace, and are more difficult to re-ink. The wear on the ribbon makes it impossible to re-ink more than a few time before scrapping the ribbon, and this type is much more likely to suffer from ribbon jams.

Ink

The ink for an inkjet machine is the most critical part of the process after the jets themselves. It must be free of suspended particles that would jam the jets, and the formulation must ensure a rapid drying time, fast enough to be dry by the time the paper moves, but wet enough to penetrate the paper.

Direct replacement of an ink cartridge with the manufacturer's spares is trouble-free but expensive, and a whole industry has grown up around supplying replacement ink cartridges and ink. Whatever course you decide to adopt, buy only from a reputable supplier. If you have only limited experience with the printer, use the manufacturer's replacements until you are confident with the printer, and then try replenishing your older cartridges.

Remember that inkjet printers use a variety of methods for inking. Some use a separate ink container that can be easily replenished, others use combined cartridges of container and jets.

Toner

Toner for laser printers can be supplied in cartridge form, possibly along with a new drum, or as a refill pack. Pouring toner is not a pleasant process if you value your lungs, and the cartridge option is a much more attractive one.

You often have a choice of manufacturer's cartridges, alternative makes, or recycled cartridges. It's difficult to say anything good about recycled cartridges, because I have never managed to print more than a few pages with any of them. If that's green, I'm a penguin. The 'clone' cartridges are better, but the genuine article is often the best value for money in the long run — and that long run often means many more pages per cartridge than the alternatives.

Paper

Paper is an important item from the cost point of view if you need to do a lot of printing. I use some 40 reams per year, and with 500 sheets per ream that could work out expensive if my printer had to use costly glossy paper.

Most laser printers can use low-cost copier paper, and anything more expensive is a waste of money. Thick paper is likely to jam in the printer because of the complicated path a sheet takes in a laser printer. Inkjet printers are very much more fussy about paper, and you should try different grades and brands before making a large order of paper.

Troubleshooting your PC

Dot matrix printers are likely to need continuous-feed paper, and this is always costly. You can buy in bulk if you use a large amount of paper, but there is no way of cutting the cost of tractor-feed paper. Sheet feeders for dot-matrix printers are expensive, so that a comparatively cheap dot-matrix printer with a sheet-feeder attached will often work out more expensive than an inkjet or laser type that is supplied with a built-in sheet feeder.

Test prints

Most printers provide for printing a test sheet, usually of all the printable characters in a standard set comprising alphabetical characters, digits, punctuation marks and some graphics shapes.

This self-test is a very valuable way of testing a new batch of paper, or for checking that the printer hardware is working, because the test print can be made even if the computer is not connected — it is produced entirely by commands in a ROM inside the printer.

If a printer self-test fails, the manual should be consulted, and if nothing is suggested, the printer will have to be returned (if under guarantee) or sent for repair.

Note that if you want to assess paper for critical purposes, such as printing CAD drawings, you should not rely on a self-test. Use a drawing that contains fine lines, shading or other features that you need to use. These test drawings will reveal differences that are not obvious when you are printing only text and simple shapes.

Software problems

Many of the common software problems with printers relate to printers used over networks, and are really network problems. There are, however, some odd problems that are not related to networks.

Most inkjet users will use the maximum possible resolution which is usually 300 dpi or more. If your inkjet printer is set for low resolution (75 to 150 dpi), you will not be able to use TrueType fonts in your text. This applies only to inkjet printers, but if you use any model of printer with the *Generic/Text only* driver, TrueType fonts cannot be used.

If you encounter problems with any of the following printers, look at the file called printers.txt in the C:\windows folder for help.

Canon Color Bubble-jet	Fargo Primera	Fargo Pro
H-P Deskjet	H-P Laserjet	H-P Color Laserjet
Lexmark	Lasermaster	NEC Silentwriter
Panasonic KX-P 6100	Panasonic KX-P 6300	Panasonic KX-P 6500

6 Software faults

Software faults are seldom so final as hardware faults, so that you can always escape by switching off. This at least allows you to switch to another program and do something else while you try to remember what you did to trigger the fault. The drawback is that when you switch off you will lose any data that you had, perhaps over several hours, typed in — unless, of course, you made backups at intervals.

Windows 95 is very much more tolerant of software faults than its predecessors, with the particular advantage that if you are running several applications, a failure of one will not bring down the others. You can leave the faulty application as it is and carry on with the others, or you can close the faulty application and continue with the others. You can expect Windows 98, and all following versions, to be even better in this respect.

When an application that runs under Windows 95 stops working correctly and locks up, you can find out what is happening by pressing the Ctrl–Alt–Del keys simultaneously. A message will appear (you might have to wait for it) that will list all the software that is running with the faulty application at the top, noting that it can be shut down or left until later. You are reminded that you can shut down the computer totally by using Ctrl–Alt–Del again.

If you take the option to shut down, the application that has caused the fault will be shut down and you will see one of your other applications on the screen. If you take the other option, to return to the situation, you will be returned to Windows so that you can switch to another application. You might think that this is not particularly useful, but it allows you to see if the cause of the delay was simply a pause while a program sorted itself out.

- The applications list that appears when you use Ctrl–
  Alt–Del will contain some names that you do not

recognise. This is because it lists **all** the files that your applications have called to provide code, not simply the main application names.

Software faults can be annoying, but if you backup your data at intervals the risk of loss is lower. Tracing the causes of software faults can be very difficult because of the huge number of possibilities that are involved. Consider, for example, how many thousands of Windows programs exist. Now think how many combinations of, say, five programs could be running together. It is quite impossible to test all of these combinations, even superficially, and equally impossible to predict what might happen when two come to a disagreement.

Some problems are well-documented, and software will be modified either to remove the problem, or to reduce the chances of it happening. This is one reason for registering your software, because if your name is not on the register, there is no possibility that you will be notified about updates or bug reports.

For sorting out obscure faults, nothing quite beats the Internet. Somewhere, someone may have encountered and solved the same fault, so that a call for help will nearly always produce some response, sometimes from people who are fascinated by problems and are determined to sort out the more interesting ones. You have to decide for yourself if knowing the cause of the problem is worth the cost of chasing it around the Internet — it could easily cost more than buying a program upgrade. It will certainly cost more than reading on and trying some of the remedies proposed here.

Memory full faults

It is unusual to get a memory full error message if you work using Windows, but this type of message is pretty familiar if you use DOS along with Windows 3.1. You might, for

Troubleshooting your PC

example, use Windows 3.1 for all of your main programs, but DOS for a few games and other assorted items.

The problem is that, no matter how much memory your computer has, DOS can use and recognise only 640 Kbyte of it, and all DOS programs are designed to run inside this memory limit. At one time, there was a system for allowing to use more memory with DOS, but this has fallen into disuse because all the large programs that are now in use run under Windows.

If you get an error message about memory, then, it is usually because you are trying to run a DOS program, and there isn't enough memory available in the first 640 Kbyte that DOS uses. You can usually get around this by shifting some of the programs that are using this memory. Most of them will be drivers, and you do not have to do the shifting for yourself, because there is a DOS utility called MEMMAKER that will do it all for you.

You must use MEMMAKER from DOS, so you need to start your computer in DOS, and then find where the MEMMAKER program is stored — it will usually be in the C:\DOS or C:\MSDOS folder on a Windows 3.1 machine.

There is no point in looking for MEMMAKER if you use Windows 95. The DOS programs are stored in the C:\windows\command folder, and MEMMAKER is not among them, because Window 95 uses different ways of allocating memory to DOS programs.

Still using DOS, switch to the folder that contains MEMMAKER and type the program name (then press ENTER). MEMMAKER will run and try to shift programs out of the first 640 Kbyte of memory. This will involve shutting down and restarting (automatically), and this may have to be done more than once. When MEMMAKER reports that it has finished, you should have more of this

68

DOS memory available, and this should solve the out of memory problems that affect your DOS programs.

No-response faults

One very common fault condition is a lock-up, when there is no response to keyboard or mouse. This is possible in almost any program, and when (not **if**) you encounter it you should first of all check that the wait is not due to what might be called natural causes.

To start with, assuming that you are using Windows 95, can you see the hourglass pointer? If this is visible, the delay might be due to normal Windows action. This is likely if you are using a computer that is too slow for the task, such as running Word 97 on a 486 machine.

- This is not infallible, and the hourglass might be visible for hours. A faulty copy of Windows Messaging, for example, will show the hourglass when you click on a message heading to see the complete message, and this display will not resolve itself — you have to escape using Ctrl–Alt–Del.

Another source of delays is the use of background operations. If you have opted to use background disc access or printing, some program actions, particularly shutting down a program, can be delayed until background actions are completed. If you disable background disc access, in particular, you will at least get some indication of when the hard drive is being used.

The most serious form of lock-up is not accompanied by any pointer. All pointers disappear, and neither the mouse nor any normal key action will have any effect. You need not sit watching for some action, because it is most unlikely you will see any, and the only course left open to you is to use the Ctrl–Alt–Del option.

- Once again, do not confuse this with slow actions. Using a computer that is much too slow for modern programs can produce similar effects, but you will soon enough know what to expect.

Illegal operation faults

Another type of software fault is caused when programs conflict and try to use each others memory space. This immediately results in an *Illegal Operation* message on the screen, so that you do not at least have to wait to find out if you have a fault.

The *Illegal Operation* panel contains a *Details* button that can be clicked for an explanation, but it is unlikely that you will be any the wiser from reading it. The explanation shows where the memory violation took place, but this is intelligible only to a programmer who knows the programs well.

The advice (from Microsoft) on the *Illegal Operation* panel is to contact the manufacturer of the software. This is not always useful, because the manufacturer may be defunct or (in my experience) is Microsoft itself. Of the last 50-odd *Illegal Operation* panels I have seen, 43 were from Word.

- Another possibility is that something else has triggered the message, and the fault is something quite different. For example, the setting of the year on the system clock can affect some programs, so that a memory violation message is triggered if the clock is set to 2097. The clock can be altered in the course of a software fault, and you might not suspect the clock or check to find what year was being stored.

The important thing to do is to note, as far as possible what you did just prior to seeing the notice. You might, for example, have just loaded a file, just tried to get to the end of a document, just tried to insert a file. These are actions that are most likely to trigger a fault, and if you write down what you did, there is a chance that you can reproduce the fault. Once you can reproduce a fault you are well on the way to solving the problem, because you will know when the fault has been cured.

- A software fault can also show up as a difference between settings and their effect. For example, if you are using Word and the screen picture shows correct page margins, but the printer prints quite different margins, then suspect a software fault in the printer driver. The remedy is to shut down completely and re-start, which should remove the problem (but watch for side-effects, such as altering the system clock settings).

Solving problems

Solving a software problem that causes either a lockup or an Illegal Operation (or General Protection Fault on Windows 3.1) notice starts, as noted above, with trying to reproduce the fault. Some faults may be impossible to reproduce, so that there is little point in worrying about them (though you might like to review your ideas on keeping backups). The fault that is most likely to be solved is one that is consistent and can be made to appear by going through a procedure that you have noted down.

Before you join others in listening to *Greensleeves* being played over and over again while you wait for a Helpline to answer, here are a few points that you can try for yourself.

If the fault occurs each time you load a file, insert a file, or try to move to the end of a file:

1 Try loading or inserting other files. If they do not trigger the fault, then the cause is just the one file.

2 Try loading a backup of the same file. If this does not trigger the fault, then your main file copy is corrupted and this is the source of the problem.

71

3   Use ScanDisk from System Tools on the file. Try loading it after ScanDisk has run. If the fault does not appear you have solved the problem, once again one of file corruption.

4   If the fault occurs each time you load or insert any file, the program itself is likely to be corrupted — see later.

If the program locks up or reports an illegal operation as soon as you load it, this points to corruption in the program itself. There are some exceptions:

1   The **order** of loading programs may be significant. For example, some Internet programs will trigger illegal operation notices if they are loaded in the wrong order.

2   Some programs will always conflict, and should never be running together. This is rare nowadays, but it can happen.

3   Programs may be affected by software that has been loaded by MS-DOS (in the CONFIG.SYS or AUTOEXEC.BAT files). This can be dealt with by the tedious course of removing commands until the problems no longer appears, but you should **not** try this unless you are familiar with MS-DOS. Lines in the CONFIG.SYS or Autoexec.bat files need not be removed; it is sufficient to edit so that the word REM is the first word in the line.

4   Program files can be corrupted. Running ScanDisk will have an effect, but it will not necessarily make the program useable again, and you will have to re-install, see later.

There are, incidentally, other conflicts that do not cause lockup or illegal operation notices, but which can be annoying. One such conflict concerns filenames, and this can have quite bizarre results.

- An example is the CAD program AutoSketch, which conflicts with another drawing program called SmartSketch. Each uses the word Sketch to start the program, and if you have both programs on the hard drive, you cannot have both running together. If SmartSketch is running, any attempt to start AutoSketch will result in starting another copy of SmartSketch. The same problem appears if you start AutoSketch first and then try to start SmartSketch.

Though you can change the filename of data files, it is most inadvisable to try to change the name of a program, because this usually makes it unworkable. The effect is rare enough, but it can be annoying if you want to copy data between these programs using the Clipboard.

Re-installation

The last resort for software problems is the re-installation of the program software. Fortunately, this is also the most successful action in most cases that have not responded to other solutions. It is not something that you should take lightly, however, because re-installing a program may have some impact on other programs, and it will certainly have some effect on data files.

Before you start re-installing a program, go through this procedure:

1   Make certain that you have the original program discs that you can use for installation. Look in particular for any serial number or registration number that you might have to type in. If you have a tape or other large-capacity backup system, back up your programs before you remove anything.

2   Look for any data files that are part of the program, and save these on a floppy. During re-installation, these may be replaced by blank files, so that you lose your data.

3   Check the effect on other programs. For example, removing Windows Messaging affects Microsoft Fax, Email and others, so that you might need to re-install more than you expected.

4   Check to see if the program is listed in the *Add/Remove Software* section of Control Panel. If it is, then remove it using this panel. This ensures the removal of files that are placed elsewhere (such as in C:\windows\system), and which might be the cause of the problem. Simply deleting the folder that holds the main program files does not necessarily delete the program entirely.

Once you have removed the offending program, re-install it. Remember that some programs, as noted above, need serial or registration numbers to be entered, and some will show messages to remind you that the program is licensed only for use on one computer at a time.

Close Windows 95 down after installation, if the act of installing has not already caused a reboot. When you start again, test the effects that caused the lockout. If the fault recurs, the Helpline is the last resort.

Registry

One very important part of Windows 95 needs to be backed up independently, because faults in this section can cause endless problems with software. The Registry of Windows 95 contains all the information on your software and its settings.

The registry of Windows 95 is a database contained in two files that should be backed up at intervals. The registry files are checked and (if necessary) altered each time the computer is shut down; this is the reason for the delay between selecting *Shut Down* and getting the message that you can finally switch off.

The registry files are called SYSTEM.DAT and USER.DAT, and are located in the C:\WINDOWS folder. There is another pair of files, SYSTEM.DA0 and USER.DA0, which are duplicate backup files located in the same folder. You should, at intervals, make copies of the DAT files on to a floppy in case of any corruption of the Registry caused by hard drive failure. Though the copies will not be up to date, they will at least contain most of the Registry information that is needed to run the computer as it was configured at the time when the backups were made.

In normal circumstances it should never be necessary to alter the Registry files directly, only by way of options within programs (such as the *File Location* options in Word). **You should not on any account alter Registry settings unless you have been advised to do so in a book or a magazine article, and only if you back up the Registry files first.** Careless alteration of the Registry files can severely restrict your use of Windows 95.

When it is necessary to edit the registry, you can either use a specialised editor (which will usually allow access only to some specific portions of the Registry) or the REGEDIT utility that is built into Windows 95. To start this editor, click on Start — Run and type REGEDIT (or click the arrowhead to see if this name is already present in the list). The *Editor* panel shows an Explorer-type of display starting with *My Computer*, and with the six main portions of the Registry displayed with their names, all starting with HKEY. Each main title carries a [+] box that indicates that you can click on the box to expand the display, and most of the HKEY entries will expand to several levels, with information held only in the lowest levels. The database main sections are illustrated in the picture of REGEDIT in action.

Of these, HKEY_CLASSES_ROOT contains information on association of data files with programs, and the sections that

Troubleshooting your PC

you are most likely to use are those that deal with current user, local machine and current configuration.

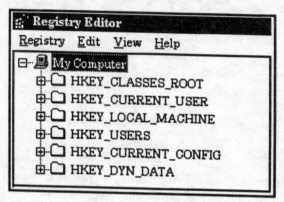

Restoration

If you do anything that scrambles the Registry information, you can return to the condition that the Registry had when you switched the computer on – this is more likely to be useful than restoring from a backup disc that might have been made some time ago. If you make a backup of the SYSTEM and USER data file before you use REGEDIT, you can use this backup to restore files in the eventuality of problems arising.

If you need to restore from the internal files, this is done by renaming the SYSTEM.DA0 and USER.DA0 files to the DAT extensions, but this **must** be done from MS-DOS rather than from Windows (since Windows may not be functioning). If you know how to use MS-DOS the procedure is fairly simple, but if you have never used MS-DOS you must follow the steps precisely.

First, use Start — Shut Down, and select the *Restart the Computer in MS-DOS Mode* option. When the machine restarts, it will be running MS-DOS, not Windows, and you need to make certain that you are using the correct folder by typing CD C:\WINDOWS (press the RETURN or ENTER

key). This assumes that your Windows files are in this folder
– use whatever drive letter and folder is appropriate for your
system.

Type each line as shown below, ending each line by pressing
the RETURN or ENTER key. The spaces are important, as
is the use of a zero in the names SYSTEM.DA0 and
USER.DA0.

    ATTRIB -H -R -S SYSTEM.DAT

    ATTRIB -H -R -S SYSTEM.DA0

    ATTRIB -H -R -S USER.DAT

    ATTRIB -H -R -S USER.DA0

    COPY SYSTEM.DA0 SYSTEM.DAT

    COPY USER.DA0 USER.DAT

You should then switch off, wait, and restart the computer.
When Windows 95 is started it will use the registry as it was
before you made any alterations.

If you have make a backup of SYSTEM.DAT and
USER.DAT to a floppy in the A: drive, you follow the
method of restarting in MS-DOS mode, and then place the
floppy in the A: drive. The MS-DOS instructions are then:

    CD C:\WINDOWS

    ATTRIB -H -R -S SYSTEM.DAT

    ATTRIB -H -R -S USER.DAT

    COPY A:*.DAT C:\WINDOWS

– remembering to press the RETURN or ENTER key. You
can then restart the computer to run Windows 95.

- From time to time, magazines issue instructions on how
  to use the Registry for actions that are not available
  from Windows. You may feel that you are never likely

to need these actions, but you should note them because if you ever need to edit the Registry you need all the help you can get.

• The REGEDIT program contains a command that allows you to export the registry files as text. This makes it possible to print the files and examine them at leisure rather than only when REGEDIT is running. These files are large, and you will need to load up with paper before you print.

Using Read-me files

Your C:\windows folder contains a large number of TXT files which are intended to deal with both software and hardware problems. Many of these deal with exotic problems that are not likely to be encountered in the UK, but some of the advice may be just what you are looking for. For example, the current (August 1997) issue of Windows 95 contains the files:

Config.txt	Display.txt	Exchange.txt
Extra.txt	Faq.txt	Faultlog.txt
General.txt	Hardware.txt	Infrared.txt
Internet.txt	Modemdet.txt	Mouse.txt
Msdosdrv.txt	Msn.txt	Ndislog.txt
Network.txt	Printers.txt	Programs.txt
Pws.txt	Readme.txt	Support.txt
Tips.txt	Winnews.txt	

Each of these files contains a large number of comments on problems, solutions and other advice, and you might want to print out the more relevant documents for quick reference. The Programs.txt pages, for example, list programs that cause problems when they are used along with the FAT32 (OSR2) version of Windows 95, and also lists other programs that will not run correctly until you obtain updated versions.

7 Hardware diagnostics and utilities

Programs that are designed to find hardware faults have been around for a considerable time, and each new version of Windows incorporates more of them. Some are run automatically as the computer is booting up, and in this chapter we shall look mainly at what is available already rather than at the programs that you can buy independently.

We have already seen that changes in the memory, hard or floppy drive or keyboard can trigger the appearance of the CMOS RAM panel, inviting you to check what has changed and either acknowledge or enter data.

Hardware problems are associated either with an addition of new hardware, removal of existing hardware, or faults in existing hardware. Under Windows 95, any new hardware that you add is likely to be to the plug'n'play (PnP) standards, ensuring that it will be recognised and correctly installed by the system with no effort required by you.

Problems are more likely to arise if you are installing an old piece of hardware, perhaps taken from an older computer, or hardware into an old computer This will not conform to PnP standards, so that it might cause conflicts. If you are using an older computer, you must be sure that any hardware that you add is suitable, because new hardware may be completely incompatible. This is particularly true for memory units and hard drives. The operative words are *may* and *might*, because many items cause no problems at all.

- If your hardware, for example, plugs into a parallel or a serial port, it is unlikely to produce any problems of conflict. Parallel port devices, such as scanners, are particularly immune from these problems.

Problems are more likely if the old hardware uses a card that has to be plugged into the computer. Such cards often contain jumpers that have to be set, and the settings will determine if any conflicts are likely. The settings are usually of address, Input/Output (I/O) and IRQ, and you should note the numbers that appear on the card or on any documentation that you have.

- You can compare these numbers (in hex code) with the numbers that are assigned to other devices when you look at the Control panel display, see later. This will indicate any conflict, and also enable you to pick numbers that are not in conflict with anything else, see later.

Modern cards do not use jumpers, so that there is nothing that can be set, and they cannot be used with a computer that does not allow plug'n'play action.

How to find where a conflict exists

You can check for hardware problems and conflicts by using the Control Panel of Windows 95 or Windows 98. This is not possible under older operating systems unless you buy additional diagnostic software, though the MSD program that was supplied with later versions of MS-DOS can be very useful.

To check your hardware using Windows, start Control Panel and proceed as follows:

1   Double-click System and click on the Device Manager Tab.

2   The set of panels that appears varies according to the device that is being checked. The first (general) panel shows Device Status, and you should see the message: *This device is working properly* if all is well.

3   For some devices, such as the Video Board, there will be a *Resources* tab. Click this to check for conflicts. You can also note the numbers that are displayed for interrupt numbers (IRQ), Input/output and memory use. For each

Troubleshooting your PC

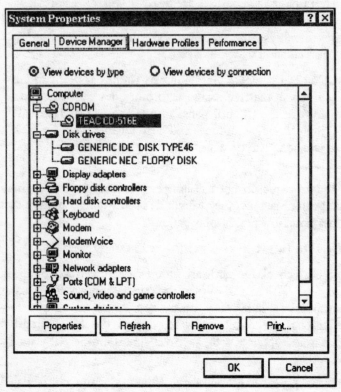

hardware class in the list, click on the [+] box to reveal the items.

4   For each item, click the name and then the Properties button.

• The devices that appear are only those that Windows 95 recognises from the PnP system. If, for example, you have added another parallel port of an older type, it will not appear in this list, though it will appear in the CMOS RAM list.

Do not be tempted to experiment with settings unless you know (perhaps from the *What's This* pointer) that you can

82

change an option. Making changes without knowing what you are doing can cripple your PC. Remember that these settings apply only to the hardware that has been installed by PnP.

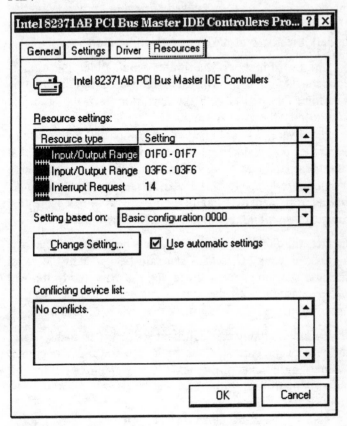

Older machines

Older machines, or machines using Windows 3.1 or DOS, are not so well served for hardware diagnosis. One useful rule is to run older machines using only the hardware (and software) that was available at the time. For example, if you are using a 386 machine, do not install a modern sound card and CD-ROM drive. You may be able to avoid hardware conflicts, but the software that you run on such a system will run painfully slowly. There is also a fair chance that the machine will have memory problems because of the driver software that has been added for these devices. Though memory can be re-organised using a program called MEMMAKER (located in the C:\DOS or C:\MSDOS folder), the action of the hardware will be slow.

As far as fitting new hardware on an older machine is concerned, you will have to make use of any installation hardware that comes with the hardware — make sure that you specify the type of computer you are using when you buy hardware. As noted earlier, hardware that makes use of a parallel port is likely to run smoothly, but hardware that uses a separate card may need jumpers to be set. These jumpers are likely to be needed for setting memory range, I/O address, and IRQ number, and you have to ensure that the settings will not conflict with other hardware.

In fact, the factory settings are often perfectly satisfactory, because if your PC is of a standard design with the usual fittings, the hardware settings for the new hardware will avoid conflicts with the standard items. Problems usually arise only if you are fitting more than one hardware item.

If you have a hardware fault, you will have to make use of the few diagnostics that are built into the older operating systems, or in the hardware itself. For example, a printer will have its own diagnostics, and should be able to print a test page. If this is possible, any fault is likely to be in the cable or connectors rather than in the printer, and diagnostic programs such as MSD can pick up any fault with the parallel port itself.

If you are using a modern PC along with an older operating system, usually Windows 3.1, you can use the MSD program for diagnostics, but you should use MSD from DOS rather than from Windows. The usual Windows 3.1 arrangement is to boot into DOS, and then run Windows by

typing the command WIN (Return). You should run MSD
before you start Windows. See later for details of MSD.

Watching the boot messages

As the PC boots, a number of messages appear on screen
before Windows 95 starts. These messages appear while
MS-DOS is loading, and you will see a summary of
hardware settings appear briefly. Unfortunately, these appear
for too short a time to take in, and there is no simple way of
capturing the messages. If, however, you always watch the
machine boot, you will be aware of any change to the
messages, which is an indication of trouble.

• Note that Windows also can deliver messages, usually
  concerning deletion of files that Windows needs or
  might need. This is often caused by deleting files
  instead of using the Uninstall facility of Control Panel
  — Add/Remove Software.

Using diagnostic software

The best-known diagnostics programs are Norton Utilities
and PC Tools. You need to ensure that the version of either
program matches the age of your computer. In particular, the
versions that were useful for Windows 3.1 are not suitable
for Windows 95, and Windows 98 might require newer
versions.

• Some of the actions of these programs are useful only if
  you understand how the PC machine uses its memory,
  and some actions can cripple your computer if you use
  them incorrectly. In general, if you are not an expert or
  working under expert advice, you should use only the
  parts that provide diagnosis or which read memory or
  the disc contents. You should avoid anything that
  writes data to the hard drive, unless this is done
  automatically as part of a routine for repairing a fault
  condition.

Troubleshooting your PC

As far as which program is more suitable, that's not an issue, because they both carry out the essential actions, and your choice might boil down to having one program bundled along with your computer, or finding one at a more attractive price. You might find, with experience that you prefer one to the other, but that's very much an individual decision.

The essential actions of such programs are:

1 To read the contents of the memory.

2 To read the data stored on the hard drive, or on other drives.

3 To backup data to floppies or tape.

4 To diagnose faults in memory or drives.

Reading the contents of memory is a way of extracting data from the memory or finding what is stored in different parts of the memory. This is not necessarily useful unless you know what you are doing, but it can sometimes be used to extract data that you had forgotten to save when you closed down a program.

Reading hard (or other) drive data can be valuable if a drive fault has made the data inaccessible. You can also use this part of the diagnostic software to read floppy discs that cannot be read by conventional means, and this can allow you to extract data from discs that were not even created using a PC, such as 3.5 inch discs created from the Amstrad PCW machines.

The backup routines of diagnostic programs can be very useful if you do not use Microsoft Backup (or if your version of Microsoft Backup is old). You can back up on floppies, or to other backup devices such as tape drives or removable hard drives. These utilities are not used to a great extent nowadays because if you buy any form of backup drive it will come with its own utilities.

The diagnosis of faults in memory or drives is the most useful action of diagnostic software and the one that is most commonly used. This is a 'peace of mind' action, because faults in memory or a hard drive are quite rare, and the point of having diagnostic software is to reassure you that whatever troubles you are experiencing, it is not due to these causes.

- A cunning variation on diagnostic programs is the 'check and fix' type. This runs continually while your computer is working and will try to sort out any faults that occur, using a floppy disc in the event of a serious failure. The later versions of Norton Utilities include this type of action.

Microsoft diagnostics and utilities

If you use Windows 95 or 98 you hardly need to buy utilities from other sources, because Windows contains three important hard drive utilities in the form of Scandisk, Defragment and Backup.

To make use of these, start Windows Explorer and click the hard drive icon. Now click on File — Properties to see general information on the drive, and click on the Tools tab to see the utilities. For each action, you will see a message that tells you when the utility was last used. Scandisk is listed under the heading of *Error-checking status*. You will see a message to tell you when you last checked the drive, and whether another check is advisable.

Scandisk use has been covered in Chapter 2, and you should remind yourself of this if you want to use Scandisk now.

Defragment appears listed as Defragmentation Status on the Tools list, and its purpose is to reorganise the drive so that it performs better.

When a file is deleted, its codes remain on the disc, but the space can from then on be used to store other files, replacing the bytes of the deleted file. If, however, the replacement files do not take up the same amount of space, there will be portions of the disc that are unused, and if a large number of files are saved, deleted and then replaced, the disc will start to suffer from fragmentation. On such a disc, saving a new file might make use of several portions of the disc that contained fragments of deleted files, and because the disc head has to move from portion to portion to read or write such a fragmented file, the time needed is longer.

A hard drive uses data units called clusters and because MS-DOS allowed for only a comparatively small number of clusters, hard drives formatted before 1997 did not use a uniform cluster size. The minimum cluster size for such drives is important, because a complete cluster will be used even if your data consists only of ten bytes. The cluster sizes (in Kbyte units) for typical hard drive sizes (in Mbyte units) on older drives are:

Drive size	Cluster size	Drive size	Cluster size
16–127	2	128–255	4
256–511	8	512–1023	16
1024–2048	32		

For the later OSR2 system used on Windows 95 in 1977, and on Windows 98, the cluster size is fixed at 4 Kbyte for all drives of less than several Gbyte capacity. This change affects many hard drive utilities, and you should take care not to use utilities that were written for MS-DOS or for earlier versions of Windows.

Defragmentation is a process that locates the fragments of files and stores them in adjacent parts of the disc, making access to such *contiguous files* quicker. To do this, files are read into memory and back to another part of the disc, and the whole process can take several hours on a large disc. Windows 98 will, in addition, reorganise a drive so that the files you use most frequently are placed where access is fastest. The display that appears shows boxes to represent file data and spaces to show unused portions of the drive.

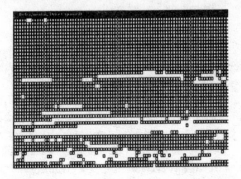

To use the defragmentation tool, close down all programs and click Start — Programs — Accessories — System Tools. Now click on **Disk Defragmenter**. You will be asked which drive you want to defragment, the default is C:\. When you select a drive and click on the *OK* button, there will be a pause while the disc is checked, and a message will tell you how fragmented the disc is, and whether defragmentation is needed. If the fragmentation is 0% then you quite certainly do not need to use the defragmenter, but you may find that a drive with a fragmentation figure as low as 3% (with defragmentation not recommended in the message) can still show a gain in speed of use after defragmentation. Click the *Start* button to start the defragmentation of the selected disc. If you are using the later OSR2 type of drive formatting (later Windows 95 and Windows 98) the process will start at once.

On older Windows 95 versions, you can click the *Advanced* button to see options for the defragmentation process itself. There are three options for the process, labelled as *Full Defragmentation (Files and Free Space)*, which is the default. The other two are *Defragment Files Only* and

Troubleshooting your PC

Consolidate Free Space Only. You can check a box to make the defragmenter check the disc for errors before defragmenting (such errors are noted, so that the faulty parts of the drive will not be used again)..

Backup is a facility that you should more frequently than the other two. Backup allows you to backup data in compressed form on floppies, tapes, other computers on a network, or removable hard drives. You can also use it to compare a backup file with the original, and to retrieve files from backed-up form. The process is automatic once started, though if you use floppies you may need to change discs at intervals – about 4 Mbyte can be saved on each floppy. Only a few types of tape drive (such as the Colorado Jumbo) are recognised by *Backup*, and if you use other types you will need to use the software that comes with the backup system.

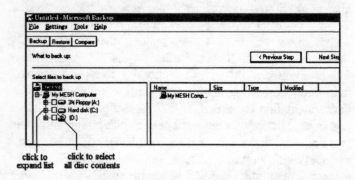

click to expand list   click to select all disc contents

To start the backup, click the *Start* button, followed by *Programs*, *Accessories* and *System Tools*. From the *System Tools* set, click *Backup*. The main *Microsoft Backup* panel will appear. The description here is for the pre-1977 version of Windows 95, but the changes that were made later do not make much difference to the way that you use the program.

Backup shows a list of folders and files in Windows Explorer format, with a small box next to each name. Click this box to place a tick into it and so select it. Selecting a drive will select all folders and files on that drive. Selecting a folder name will select for backup all the files in that folder. You can also select file names individually. If a large number of files is selected the process can take several minutes.

When files have been selected, you can click the *Next Step* button. This selects a destination for the backup, and the two most likely are **floppy drive** or (if you have a tape backup) **tape**. Make sure that a blank floppy or tape is inserted into the drive, and then click the *Start Backup* button. You will be asked to type a filename for your backup, and a useful type of filename is the date (such as 8JUN96) along with an indication of the contents (DATA, SYSTEM, PROGS, etc.). When you have done this the backup will start. If you are using floppies you will be prompted to change discs at intervals. You should label these floppies in sequence, as they will need to be inserted in the same order when you restore the contents.

If you are likely to back up the same selection several times, you can save it as a file set. This is particularly useful if you have selected several folders, because if the contents of the folders change, they will still be automatically selected for backup because the folder has been selected. The File set can be saved after you have selected a destination for the backup by clicking File — Save As in the menu, and providing a filename for the selection. This is saved as a file of type SET and can be obtained subsequently by using File — Open File Set the next time you make a backup.

A file set for *Full System Backup* (FSB) is provided and can be loaded in when you are asked to select files. An FSB will backup all of the files on the hard drive, including the important Windows registry files, so that you should make at least one backup of this type if you have a tape drive or a removable hard drive (the size of the FSB makes it unlikely that you will want to use floppies for this purpose). You can decrease the size of the FSB set by removing from it all data files and, if necessary, all program files other than the Windows set. You will be asked to confirm any change to the FSB set.

The Settings — Options menu allows you to specify options for general use and for the three main actions of Backup, Restore and Compare. These are detailed below:

General: The options boxes provide for turning on audible prompts and for overwriting old status log files. Both of these can normally be ticked, unless there is some particular reason for retaining old log files.

Backup. The main option box is labelled *Quit Backup after operation is finished,* and this can be ticked if you want to resume normal working as soon as possible after making a backup. You can also choose between making a full backup on all selected files and making an incremental backup only of files that have changed since the last full backup. See later for details of incremental backup.

The *Advanced* section has four option boxes. The *Verify backup* data box will automatically carry out a file comparison between the backup copy and the original and report on any differences. The box labelled *Use Data Compression* should be ticked, particularly if you are backing up to floppies, as it makes full use of the available storage space. The option to *Format if necessary on tape backup* provides for using unformatted tape. The option of *Always erase on tape backup* allows the same tape to be used over and over again for a full backup, and must not be used if you want to make incremental backups on the same tape. The last option is *Always erase on floppy disc backup,* and this also is usually desirable unless you want to avoid the possibility of wiping a disc by mistake.

Restore. As for Backup, the main option is the *Quit Restore after operation is finished,* and you will probably want to tick this option. You can also choose whether to restore backup files to the *Original location* (the default), to an *alternative location*, or to an *alternative location, into a single folder (directory)*. The use of an alternative location allows you, for example, to place all of your files on a new hard drive (added in parallel with the original), and the use of a single folder allows a set of files to be restored from a backup so that you can find them all without having to search through a set of folders.

The *Advanced* section provides for verifying restored data against the backup copy, and the options for files of the same name are *Never overwrite files, Overwrite older files only*, or *Overwrite files*. If you use this last option you can opt for a prompt message each time a file is to be overwritten.

Compare. The *Quit after operation is finished* option is used in this set also. The file comparison options are *Original location, Alternate location*, and *Alternate location, single folder (directory)*.

The other options provide for *Drag and Drop* and for *File Filtering*. The *Drag and Drop* options allow you to specify how you want Backup to proceed when you have the Backup program displayed as an icon and you have selected files and dragged them to the Backup icon. The options are to *Run Backup Minimized*, to *Confirm Operation before Beginning*, and to *Quit after Backup is Completed*. *File filtering* allows you to specify file types (in the form of extension letters) that you want to exclude from a backup, or to exclude files on the basis of date.

You can opt for full or incremental backup of the files you have selected. A *Full backup*, as the name suggests, backs up the files completely, so that they can be restored to the state they were in at the time of the backup. An *Incremental backup* can be made only following a full backup of the same files, and it backs up only the changes in files. This action should be reserved for specialised purposes, because it does not back up new files that have been added to folders, only changes in files that were previously backed up. You must clear the *Always Erase on Tape Backup* option box before you add an incremental backup to a tape that contains an existing full backup. When you recover files, both the full backup and the incremental backup must be present.

MSD

MSD is Microsoft Diagnostics, and running this program will provide a printout of the state of your computer. This program is not included in your Windows System Tools set, and is not present at all in computers sold from mid-1977 onwards. If you have a folder called \DOS or \MSDOS then you will probably find MSD in that folder. You should run MSD from DOS rather than from Windows. You do not need MSD if you are using Windows 95 or Windows 98, because the information is available in the System portion of Control Panel. MSD is needed if you use only DOS or Windows 3.1.

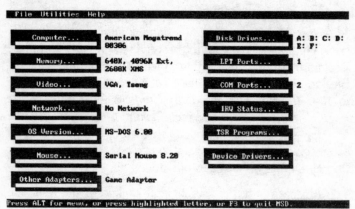

You can look at the MSD report on or send the report to a disc file for printing out directly or by using a word-processor. There are three file report options depending on how you want the data organised. The straightforward command MSD produces a summary of headings:

Computer   Drives   Memory

LPT Ports   Video COM Ports

Network   IRQ Status   OS Version

TSR Programs   Mouse   Device drivers

Other Adapters

You can gain additional information on each of the topics shown here by clicking the mouse with the cursor over the topic on which you want more information. The information under the heading of *Computer* will be information on the BIOS chip for any PC clone.

The *Memory* option will show a summary of the use of memory in the range from 640 Kbyte to 1024 Kbyte — this is shown in two screens, using the scroll bar at the side to move from one to another, and the illustration shows the upper part. The TSR option (Terminate and Stay Resident programs) lists programs that remain in the memory while the computer is running (such as drivers) and indicates how each TSR uses the lower portion of the memory.

8 Adding hardware

Computer equipment becomes out of date almost as soon as you have bought it. That's something you have probably found out if you have owned a computer before now, and it's certainly something that you will discover if you are currently using your first computer.

Now if your computer continues to do what you bought it to do, and you don't think you need more speed, more memory, or more hard drive space, then carry on by all means. There is no point in upgrading if you don't need to, and the low price of second-hand computers is partly due to the number of people who update needlessly.

The crunch comes, however, if you buy new software. Each new generation of software, each upgrade of a word-processor, database, spreadsheet, etc., needs faster processing, more memory, more hard drive space. There seems no end to it, and if your computer uses a P166 Pentium, 32 Mb of RAM and a 2.5 Gb hard drive, you may find it difficult to believe that only ten years ago we thought it sufficient to have a plain 8086 processor with 640 Kb of RAM, and no hard drive, or (for the more advanced) a 32 Mb hard drive.

There are times when the only way of updating a system is to buy a completely new machine, but if your machine is not totally out of date, it's a lot cheaper and more satisfactory to upgrade the hardware items that need upgrading. A second-hand computer is worth less in percentage terms than a second-hand car, but components are relatively cheap, and by upgrading you have the satisfaction of keeping the familiar machine and not having to adjust a new one to the way that you work.

If you have been using the computer for some time, you will have configured Windows just the way you want it, you will have your favourite programs on the hard drive, and you probably don't want to go through all the hassle of setting up a new machine from scratch. This makes hardware upgrading very attractive, and you are most likely to need it when you have just been doing some software upgrading, installing the latest version of your favourite software just to find that it runs too slowly or takes up too much space on your hard drive.

- You can also apply this thinking to software. If your software does what you want of it, is it worth changing to a new version that will run more slowly?

Checking what is possible

Some upgrades require very little effort. If you want to upgrade a printer, for example, you simply unplug the old printer and plug in the new one. You then have to use Control Panel of Windows 95 to add the new printer. That sounds simple enough, and it is if your new printer is a model that was in production at the time when you installed Windows 95.

If you upgrade to a new type of printer, one that was **not** available when Windows 95 was installed, then this model will not appear on the printer list of Control Panel. You then have two options. One is to look at the list of available printers and choose a similar model from the same manufacturer. The other option is to use a floppy disc supplied by the printer manufacturer.

When you use the *Add Printer* option of the *Printers* folder in Control Panel, this starts a Wizard. On the page that contains the list of manufacturers and models, there is a button labelled *Have disk*. Click this if you have a floppy disc from the printer manufacturer, and the Wizard will install the software from the disc. Once this has been installed, you can make this printer the default and you should be able to use it just as you used your old printer.

Troubleshooting your PC

Adding a modem is very similar to adding a printer if the modem is external. You have to make connections to the serial port of the computer, to the telephone socket, and to a power supply, and then use Control Panel to install the modem. Adding an internal modem is more difficult, and details follow.

Replacing a keyboard can sometimes be a useful upgrading if you do not like the keyboard that you are using. The snag is that you can seldom try out a new keyboard before buying, and this is really essential because no-one can describe the feel of a keyboard to you.

Adding a new monitor (usually a larger one) is usually straightforward, but you have to be certain that your existing graphics card will drive the monitor correctly.

In general, if added hardware requires connection to a serial or a parallel port, the process should be straightforward, and problems arise only if you do not have enough ports. For example, if you add an external hard drive (for backup) that connects to a parallel port, and you have only one parallel port that is connected to a printer, you may be able to use a connector that allows both hardware items to share the port. If this is not possible, you will need to add a second parallel port. This is straightforward enough, but it requires you to open up the computer, see later.

The most common internal upgrades are of memory and drives. It's unlikely nowadays that you would buy a computer with no CD-ROM drive, but you might have thought a year ago that you didn't need one. Similarly, a few computers are still being sold with an inadequate hard drive size, or with memory of only 8 Mbyte, and these are the machines that will have problems with modern software.

If your computer has half of its hard drive unused, you can feel reasonable confident that you do not need to upgrade the drive for some time. Most users, however, can benefit from upgrading memory. As we noted earlier, 8 Mbyte of memory is simply not adequate for modern programs, even if some manufacturers are still supplying machines with this amount, and you will see speed benefits from adding memory even if you are using 32 Mbyte.

Avoiding trouble

Hardware upgrades are straightforward actions, simpler than changing the oil on a car, but you need to check that what you are adding is suitable. At one time, the design of the PC type of computer was so standardised that you could be certain that an upgrade you bought would be suitable. Nowadays, the rate of change means that some parts are suitable and others are not, and you have to check carefully. As always, you will pay more for hardware additions if your computer carries a famous name (and some famous names try their best to make upgrading difficult).

Memory additions in particular need some care, because there are so many varieties of memory unit. The most recent types of computers are likely to use memory units called EDO or DIMM, and though some computers have sockets for both types, you may find that only one or the other, not both, can be fitted.

If, for example, your computer uses two 16 Mbyte EDO units to provide 32 Mbyte of RAM, you can expand to a total of 64 Mbyte by adding another two such units. If the computer also has two DIMM sockets, you can use these only if you remove the EDO units, and you will find that this makes the expansion much more expensive. On the other hand, if the price of 16 Mbyte DIMM units drops, and larger units become available, this might at some future time be a better way to expand.

Another item to watch is that you are buying modern equipment to add on. For example, it is useful to add a second parallel port to your computer, because this allows you to use several pieces of equipment that plug into a parallel port and which need no special installation methods. If you use an old design of parallel port card, however, you might have some difficulty in making your computer recognise it. As long as the second port appears in the CMOS RAM page, it should work, but you will probably find that it never appears in the list of hardware that is used by the Control Panel — System pages.

In general, all cards that you add on should conform to modern PnP (Plug'n'Play) standards. This ensures that there will be no conflicts caused by adding these cards, and it dispenses with the need to set jumpers or switches on the cards themselves.

Even if a piece of hardware needs no special installation methods (because it is connected through the parallel port, for example) this does not mean that it will be trouble-free, because older designs can still cause problems, particularly with hardware that was designed in the days before Windows 95. Just to take one example, one (excellent) scanner that connects through the parallel port needs to use Windows Write when you opt to read a document with the scanner. Under Windows 95, this tries to load WordPad and fails (because of a file called Write that loads WordPad). The remedy is to remove WordPad and install an old copy of Windows Write from a backup disc that was made using Windows 3.1.

You may feel that you are unlikely to buy old equipment that might cause such problems, but it's not so simple as that. There is a lot of hardware that has remained unsold from several years ago, and someone is going to buy it. For anyone using a computer that is of the same vintage this is good news because the older add-on boards should be attractively priced. If you are using a very recent machine, however, you should be very fussy about the date of manufacture of hardware that you add to your system.

Plugging in cables

One of the main causes of problems following the installation of a new board inside a computer is incorrect location of a cable plug at the end of a data cable. If you have made any changed that involved fitting of refitting a data cable, this is the usual suspect if you find problems. A typical example is the data cable to a floppy drive. If this is incorrectly attached you get symptoms such as the drive light remaining on, but no reading or writing, or the drive not being recognised in the CMOS RAM.

Data cables are marked to show which way round they go. The marking is in the form of a coloured stripe at one end of the cable, and this indicates the side of the cable (and connector) for pins 1 and 2. This end of the connector has to be turned so that it engages with the connector on the board that has the numbers 1 and 2 printed on the board.

This, however, is not all of the story, because even with the connector turned the correct way round the pins may not be engaging correctly. It is very easy, for example, to have the plug displaced so that two pins at one end are not engaged, or even with one complete line of pins not making contact.

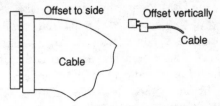

This is unlikely if you can see both connectors clearly, but you seldom can, and on many computers you can barely touch some connectors, let alone see what is happening. It helps if the connectors are 'keyed', meaning that one pin is removed from the plug and one hole from the socket, so that any mis-alignment will mean that you are trying to put a pin into a missing hole. This works if you realise that the

101

problem is not just a tightly-fitting connector — given enough force, any plug will go into any socket.

One useful hint is to mark all existing connections. If you use Tippex or some other marking fluid to identify the matching ends of plugs and sockets, this can considerably speed up re-assembly if you have had to disturb connections. If a connection is inaccessible, you may find it quicker to remove an obstruction (such as an adapter card) rather than struggle to reach and see the socket.

Above all, plan out what you are doing. Never start a job on the principle of 'seeing how it goes'. If you know exactly what to expect, and what you have to do you are much less likely to be diverted by minor problems.

Cards and drives

Card and drive addition or replacement is not a difficult task on modern computers, and is something that many owners tackle as a matter of course. The main reasons for working with drives are to replace a hard drive, add a second hard drive, or to add a CD-ROM drive or a tape backup drive. We'll look first at adding or replacing cards (boards).

Ever since the IBM PC machine was devised, its capabilities could always be enhanced by add-on cards or boards. Modern machines come with a large range of built-in facilities, and you would not need to add, for example, a graphics board or a hard-drive card to modern machines, but there are always other desirable add-ons which require boards to be inserted into the PC.

Many types of add-on cards plug into the EISA bus, which is the descendant of the old AT bus of the PC — older machines use the ISA (Industry Standard architecture) bus with which the extended version, EISA, is compatible. This uses sockets that allow for short cards (36 pins) or long cards (62 pins) to be plugged in, and you will see a gap in the sockets separating the two sections.

Typical short cards might include a parallel-port card, if you wanted to add another port; a sound card is a typical long card. Your manual should show clearly the location of these slots, but even if you do not have this information it is not difficult to match up the slot appearance with that of the card you propose to insert. Modern computers use only a few of these EISA slots, because the signals on such slots are at a slow rate, and they are used only for cards whose speed is not important.

Local bus cards work at much higher speeds than the ISA type of connection, and use a different plug-in arrangement. The two main types of local bus that have been used to date are labelled as VLB and PCI., and the VLB type are used on the older 386 and 486 machines. Pentium (and above) computers currently use the PCI type of bus. Add-on cards will be intended either for VLB or PCI and these are **not** interchangeable. If, for example, you replace a 486 motherboard by a Pentium motherboard, you normally cannot use the old graphics card on the new board because it will almost certainly be a VLB type, and the Pentium motherboard will require a PCI connection.

Some Pentium motherboards incorporate the hard drive circuits, so that you do not need to take up a PCI slot with a driver board, and a few motherboards may also incorporate a graphics card, though it is more usual to use the PCI bus for this to allow you more choice of graphics cards. Add-on cards for TV or video uses will need to use the PCI slots.

Whatever type of card is used, you start by switching off and removing the power plug from its socket. Open the computer and find the slot that you intend to use for the card. Remove the blanking plate from the back of the computer. Locate the connectors of the card over the socket and check that they are aligned, then press the card slowly and carefully into place. When the card is fully home, replace the fixing screw that was used for the blanking plate so that it holds the card in place – do not over-tighten this screw.

Drives

Fitting a drive into place, whether floppy, hard, CD-ROM or backup, is a simple operation that will cause no problems to anyone who ever used a Meccano set. Installation is automatic for a floppy drive, but it can be less straightforward for the other types if you are using an old computer (before Windows 95).

All fitting starts with the computer switched off, power plug removed, and lid lifted or cover(s) removed depending on the design of the casing. A hard drive can be fitted in a 'blind bay', one that has no opening; floppy, backup and CD-ROM drives must use a bay whose front panel can be removed to allow access to the front of the drive.

You need to have a drive bay free. For a 3½" floppy drive you need either a 3½" bay, or a 5¼" bay with an adapter. CD-ROM and backup drives can usually fit in a 5¼" bay. Make sure that the drive comes with the fixing screws, which are either 6-32 UNC × 0.31 or metric M4 × 0.7-6H. Drives sold in the UK usually come with the metric bolts, and the casing of the drive may be stamped **M** for metric or **S** for UNC. If an adapter is to be used, fasten the drive into the adapter before fixing the adapter into the computer. You may find it easier to connect the power and data cables, see below, before fixing the drive into place.

The drive must be fixed using its sprung mounting pads — this is particularly important for a hard drive. Do not on any account drill new fixing points into the drive. The drive should rest on the brackets within the bay, and should line up with four of the holes in the side of the bay so that the fixing bolts can be inserted. Hard drives do not need to be accessible from outside, so that the bay cover can remain in place (very often a bay for a hard drive will not have any cover, and may be placed anywhere inside the casing). Remove the cover if you are installing a floppy, CD-ROM or backup drive, since access is needed for inserting media.

Once the drive is in place and connected electrically, the fixing bolts can be tightened, taking care not to impose undue force on the drive. The cover for the casing can then be replaced (on a desktop casing, this means simply shutting the lid), and the power plug replaced. See Chapter 2 for a picture of a typical hard drive.

All drives require a data connection and a power connection. The power connectors emerge from the power supply box, and most cases provide a generous number, 6 to 8 usually. The power plug can be fitted only one way round. The data plug for a floppy drive is one of a pair on a cable coming (usually) from the motherboard, and the drive will be recognised as A: or B: depending on which connector is used. The data plug for a hard drive is taken from the IDE drive card, or from the motherboard directly, and usually also provides for two drives. A CD-ROM drive will either use a data cable connected to a sound card, a data cable to an adapter card, or one of the hard drive connectors. The number of hard drive connectors that can be used depends on whether you have an EIDE or IDE interface — the more modern EIDE type permits up to four connectors to be used. A backup drive may use a floppy drive data connector or an interface of its own — see the backup drive manual for details.

The data connector (on the drive) uses two close-spaced rows of connecting pins, and care is needed to ensure that all the pins are aligned with the corresponding sockets on the cable connector. The data cable has a coloured stripe at one edge to mark the Pin 1 side, and this must be aligned with the Pin 1 marker on the drive connector. If this is observed, the only remaining problem is of correctly aligning the pins with the sockets — it is remarkably easy to insert just one row of pins leaving the other set unconnected.

A new (not replacement) floppy drive will be recognised automatically, and you will see the CMOS RAM display when you switch on, allowing you to fill in details of the new drive. If you have simply replaced an existing drive, the CMOS RAM screen should not appear. Fitting a new hard drive will also cause the CMOS RAM display to appear so that you can fill in (or confirm) the information for that drive. This may also be needed if you have replaced a hard drive with one that is not electrically identical. Software will usually be provided with a CD-ROM or backup drive to ensure that it is recognised and a drive letter allocated.

- If a drive is not recognised and does not work, the main item to check is the data connector. If this seems to be in order, the installing software or CMOS RAM settings may be incorrect.

If you are adding a **second** hard drive, you will need to check the manuals for **both** hard drives. The jumpers of the original drive, the one that you boot from, will need to be set so that this is the master drive of the two, and the added drive will need its jumpers set as the slave of the two. You can then add the new drive, plugging in the data and power connectors as noted earlier. Note that this usually means that you have to remove the first hard drive to set its jumpers, and you should take great care not to confuse the drives if they are of identical types.

Internal modem

An internal modem can be plugged into an EISA slot like a card, but because the modem is a thicker unit you might find that you need to choose the position carefully, or rearrange other cards. For most modems, you need only plug the unit into place, because the default jumper settings will be suitable, but if you are using a phone-modem (that allows digital voice messages to be sent and received) you will want to set the jumpers to connect with your sound card and microphone, or with a separate loudspeaker. You will need to look at the connection guide for the modem to be sure.

• Modem manuals are often aimed at programmers, showing all the codes that the modem can obey. You do not need to pay any attention to these details, because the modem is controlled completely by your software, so that only connections are of interest.

Adding memory

The main memory of a modern PC machine is in the form of dynamic RAM, using chips on SIMM boards. SIMM means Single Inline Memory Module, and the board contains a set of memory chips connected so that plugging the board into a socket will link up all of the memory chips.

At one time, there was only one type of SIMM board with 30 pins, but in recent years several different types of board have come into use, so that it is vitally important to find which type your computer uses. Adding an incorrect type of board can cause trouble, and the added memory will certainly not work correctly. Modern SIMM boards use 72 pins. In particular, you need to know if your computer uses 8-bit or 9-bit memory SIMMs.

Currently, the most-used type of memory is called EDO (extended data output). This uses a 72-pin SIMM construction, but the memory chips are organised in a different way to provide faster action than is possible using the older plain SIMMs. The later SDRAM boards use a 168-pin connection, and are not physically interchangeable with SIMM boards. There are also DIMM boards using 72-pin connections and not compatible with other 72-pin SIMMs. Check very carefully what your motherboard requires before ordering additional memory. The computer manual will state the memory type, and any restrictions (such as not mixing different types) that you need to observe.

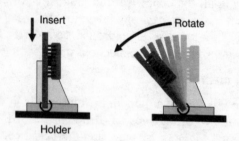

Each SIMM or EDO board is inserted into a holder which can then be turned so that the board is locked into place. Other types of memory use different insertion methods, and because new methods are constantly being devised, you should follow the instructions in the manual.

CMOS-RAM screen

The CMOS RAM, noted also in Chapter 2, is a small portion of memory on the motherboard of your computer that holds essential information that the computer needs when it starts up. Like all RAM, the CMOS RAM would lose its data if it lost power, so that a backup battery is used to keep the CMOS RAM (and the real-time clock) active while the computer is switched off.

You can check the contents of the CMOS RAM when you switch on the computer. Each motherboard type uses a different method of switching to the CMOS RAM display, usually requiring two keys to be held down as you switch on the computer. For example, some *AWARD* BIOS motherboards will switch to the CMOS RAM settings if you hold down the Ctrl, Alt and S keys together while the computer is booting up (or if you press this key combination while you are using MS-DOS). You will have to find for yourself what key combination is used for your own motherboard.

The contents of the CMOS RAM vary from one motherboard to another, but typical contents include settings for time, date, floppy drives used, hard drives used, base memory, extended memory, video card, keyboard and processor clock speed. There will also be a page of advanced settings which you should not alter unless you really know what you are doing.

Some day, the battery that backs up the CMOS RAM will fail, though the more recent types are likely to have a life of ten years or more and you will probably have upgraded your computer long before you experience a battery failure. If you have bought a second-hand machine, or if you have had a computer for a long time, you might possibly experience battery failure. If this happens, you will see the CMOS RAM screen appear when you boot up, and you will have to restore the settings before you can use the computer. This makes it very important to make a note of the settings.

There are utility programs (many of them free) which will read the CMOS RAM contents and write them back if there is a failure. If you feel that this is an excessive precaution you should at least note the essential details that appear on the main CMOS screen. In particular you should note the figures for the hard drive(s), under the heading of Cyl, Hd, Sec and Size, because unless these are correct, the computer may use only part of the hard drive, and in the worst case might not be able to read the hard drive, making it impossible to run MS-DOS or Windows from the hard drive.

Troubleshooting your PC

- In the event of battery failure, you need to replace the battery on the motherboard before you restore the CMOS RAM settings, otherwise you will have to type in the settings each time you switch on the computer.

New hardware: When you install certain types of new hardware, such as a new hard drive (replacing an older one, or adding a second hard drive), the CMOS RAM screen will appear automatically when you next switch on the computer. On older machines, you will have to fill in the details for the new hardware, and for a hard drive this means the Cyl (number of cylinders), Hd (number of heads), Sec (sector size) and Size (size in Mbytes) for that drive. These figures will be printed in the manual that comes with the new hard drive. If you buy a second-hand hard drive, make sure that you have a manual or at least a note of these numbers. For example, an 814 Mbyte hard drive would (typically) appear as:

Cyl	Hd	Sec	Size
1654	16	63	814

You will also see the automatic appearance of the CMOS RAM settings if you alter the amount of memory in your computer by adding more SIMMs. Once again, on the older machines you may need to type in the figure, but it is much more likely that this will appear automatically, and you need only check it. Most modern computers will insert even the hard drive figures automatically in to the CMOS RAM, so that the appearance of the screen is only to remind you that there has been a change, and that you can check the new settings.

Appendices

A: Startup disc

A startup disc is a floppy that can be used to boot your computer when it will not boot from the hard drive. The files on the startup disc are the minimum that can make the computer useable, and they run MS-DOS, not Windows. Once you have started the computer running MS-DOS, however, you may be able to start Windows.

The startup disc is created as follows:

1. Put a new formatted floppy into its drive.

2. Click Start — Settings — Control Panel and double-click *Add/Remove Programs*. When the panel appears, click on the *Startup Disk* tab.

3. Follow the instructions that appear.

The floppy that this creates will start the machine in MS-DOS when you boot or reboot with the floppy in place. This assumes that you have not disabled the action of booting from a floppy. If you have disabled floppy booting you need to run the CMOS RAM program, which is independent of MS-DOS or Windows, and change the settings to enable the option of checking the floppy drive for boot files.

B: Making use of magazines

One way of obtaining help, if the topic is not urgent, is by way of the computer magazines. There are many magazines available that run a set of Help pages in which you can place a query that will be answered by other readers or by the staff of the magazine. Look, for example, in PC Answers or PC Plus to see the type of problems and solutions that turn up.

If you subscribe to a magazine that has Help pages, start a scrapbook of these pages. Do not save simply the items that are of immediate interest to you because you may need some of the other items when you add hardware or change your computer.

Some magazines issue a disc at intervals that contains an index of topics. This can be useful, but such discs only provide references to articles in the magazine, so that you have to keep a bulky pile of magazines to make effective use of the disc.

C: Internet support

Microsoft maintains a large number of Internet facilities that are useful for advice on problems, both well-known and obscure. Where you see a FAQ section for frequently-asked questions, always try this first, because this is more likely to contain the information you want than the more esoteric departments. Many of the problems that are encountered concern the use of hardware and/or software that is not available in the UK, so that it is often pointless as well as time wasting to chase every reference to a problem.

If your Internet provider is MSN, the Microsoft facilities that are directly available to you include the Knowledge Base of more than 50,000 articles and the Software Library of free software (drivers, updates, bug fixes, etc.). If you use a different provider you will have to make use of the web addresses listed below.

http://www.microsoft.com/windows

This is the Windows home page, and contains a link to the Windows 95 Support Options page for downloading tools and diagnostics such as Support Assistant, Windows 95 System Check, Application Compatibility List, Hardware Compatibility List and others.

http://www.microsoft.com/kb

This is the home page for the Knowledge Base, allowing you access to the database that is used by the Help line providers.

WinNews

This is a twice-weekly bulletin that is available on Email to you, providing new information on Windows 95. To subscribe, send an Email to *enews35@microsoft.nwnet.com*. Your Email text (in the main body of the message, not Subject) must include the phrase *Subscribe WinNews*.

INDEX

Troubleshooting your PC

118

Index

Notes

Notes

Notes

Notes

Notes

Notes

Notes